To Dorothy

The Main Road

from Soldier to Songwriter

George Main

The Stewart Press

THE MAIN ROAD

ISBN 0 9523957 0 3

First Publication in Great Britain

PRINTING HISTORY
Stewart Press edition published 1994

Published by The Stewart Press
2a Queen's Avenue, Birchington, Kent CT7 9QN.

Typeset in 11pt Plantin
by Camtec, Birchington, Kent.

Printed and bound in Great Britain by The Island Press, Birchington, Kent.

CONTENTS

Chapter 1   The Beginning ....*Page 7*

Chapter 2   The Seaside..*Page 15*

Chapter 3   The Church ....*Page 25*

Chapter 4   One Man's War ....*Page 31*

Chapter 5   Marriage and Suburbia..*Page 39*

Chapter 6   Sidelines..*Page 47*

Chapter 7   Home and Abroad..*Page 55*

Chapter 8   Far Away Places ....*Page 67*

Chapter 9   Retirement ....*Page 75*

Chapter 10   Man of Music..*Page 79*

Appendix 1   "Task Force" ....*Page 93*

Appendix 2   "Birchington-on-Sea" ....*Page 95*

Appendix 3   "Thanet Forever" ....*Page 97*

Appendix 4   "Circus Boy"..*Page 99*

Appendix 5   "A Children's Carol" ....*Page 101*

Appendix 6   "To My Daughter" ....*Page 103*

Appendix 7   "To My Father" and "The Christening"........*Page 105*

Appendix 8   "Sara" ....*Page 107*

Appendix 9   "To Dorothy With Love" ....*Page 109*

Appendix 10 "Golden Wedding" ....*Page 111*

Appendix 11 "The Probus Song" ....*Page 113*

Appendix 12 "Piccolo Pete and the Band" ....*Page 115*

Appendix 13 "I Wanna Go 'Ome" ....*Page 117*

1

The Beginning

That I was born at all is something of a miracle. My parents were in
their late twenties when they married in 1916 after a long courtship,
as was the custom. Although my mother came from a large family she was
woefully ignorant of the facts of life. There seemed to be something
shameful in being an expectant mother in those days, and as soon as her
pregnancy began to show my mother never left the house until after dark
to go for a short walk. My birth must have been a horrific experience for
her (although everything went well) and I was destined to be an only
child. My poor father must have suffered a life of sexual frustration,
unlike my maternal grandfather who died, presumably from exhaustion,
at the early age of forty-seven, after fathering no less than ten children.
My grandmother had become pregnant roughly every eighteen months
and was rewarded for her part in the proceedings by being allowed to stay
in bed for a whole month after the birth of each child. She lived until she
was eighty, so it couldn't have done her much harm.

I was thoroughly spoilt from the very beginning. My mother was over-
protective, living in constant fear that the midwife would fall asleep and
let me roll off her capacious lap. As a baby, I shared my parents' bed and
my mother spent many sleepless nights afraid that I would be suffocated,
but needless to say I survived; babies are tougher than one would think.
The three-storey house in North London where I was born was home not
only to me and my parents but also to my maternal grandmother and two
maiden aunts. At one time we also had a married aunt and her two small
children living with us while her husband, a petty officer in the Royal
Navy, was away at sea. However, for most of the time I was the only child in
the household and there was no shortage of devoted slaves to amuse me.

I first saw the light of day just after the end of the first World War, a
member of the lower working class. My father was poor but honest,
completely lacking in ambition. Having once been unemployed for a

short while, his sole aim was to keep his job and maintain my mother and me. He worked a five-and-a-half day week, leaving home at seven in the morning and returning at about six-thirty. To save time in the morning, he washed and shaved overnight, and crossed London by bus, sustained only by a meagre breakfast of bread, butter and golden syrup. He worked as an engineer storekeeper for a firm of lift manufacturers. The work was physically demanding and involved him standing around all day on damp stone floors, resulting in him suffering from rheumatism in later years. In common with most married men at that time, he was poorly paid and barely managed to make ends meet. My mother did not go out to work since this would have hurt my father's pride. However, we managed to exist, although I suspect that my mother made many sacrifices to keep it that way.

Our house was in De Beauvoir Road, a mis-nomer if ever there was one, located in a somewhat run-down area of North London. Most of the dwellings were terraced, with no garages of course, as cars were a rarity. For the most part the traffic consisted of horse-drawn vehicles and public transport. I remember how proud I used to feel when one of my uncles, who lived some twenty miles away and owned a furniture and removal business, visited us and parked his Morris Minor in the road outside our house. Generally, life was fairly routine with not much excitement. The milkman called daily, pushing a heavy churn. He delivered the milk to our front door in a metal container, from which it was ladled into a jug which we had to provide. The only bottled milk available was sterilised. Groceries were mostly ordered weekly and delivered on foot by a hunchback with a large wicker basket slung over his shoulder. There were occasional forays to Sainsburys, where butter was shaped into portions with wooden patters and ham was sliced from the bone. Our meat could not have been fresher. Live sheep were delivered to our local butcher and driven across the pavement to be slaughtered on the premises. Domestic refrigerators were almost unknown. At a nearby dairy, owned by a Welsh family, several cows were housed in a barn under conditions which would not be allowed these days. Fruit and vegetables were available from a sizeable hand-pushed barrow which made a daily excursion along our street. Bakers shops abounded, offering all kinds of attractive products

Charles and Elizabeth, George's parents

from crusty cottage loaves to fancy cakes. Everything seemed to be reasonably priced, but since the average household weekly income was just two or three pounds this was not surprising. On Sundays, the muffin man patrolled the streets, ringing a handbell to attract attention. My mother withdrew her patronage from him after seeing him wipe his nose on the cloth covering his wares. The streets were lit by gas lamps ignited at dusk by a lamplighter. Despite the evidence of weather reports to the contrary, almost every day of the Summer holidays seemed warm and full of sunshine. It did not get dark until about eleven o'clock, and I remember being unable to get to sleep for the noise of radios blaring from open windows. November was notorious for thick yellow fogs, and on occasions all traffic was brought to a complete halt. My wife remembers standing at her front garden gate handing out candles to passers-by unable to find their way. Every few years, workmen arrived to re-surface the roads. They sprayed tar everywhere and coated it with fine shingle. I suffered many a cut knee after falling over in the newly-surfaced road. In those days, boys wore short trousers until the age of fourteen, thus our knees were unprotected. At night the road mending equipment was guarded by a watchman of indeterminate age who sat in a wooden hut warmed by a coke brazier. Vandalism on any scale was unheard of at that time. Most households relied on gas or coal for heating and cooking. It was not until the mid-thirties that our house was wired for electricity, a great step forward. The advent of this new fuel nearly led to my demise. One day, shortly after its installation, I experimented by plugging a length of flex into a lampholder, switching on the current and trying to attach the other end of the wire to the base of an electric bulb. Inevitably, the wires touched, there was an enormous flash and all the lights went out. My father was furious, and I narrowly escaped a thrashing, but at least I survived.

Our rent was £1.00 weekly, and this was collected every month by the landlord and his wife, a couple who bore a strong resemblance to King George V and Queen Mary. In fact, they were treated like royalty by my mother, who served them tea in our lounge, or parlour as it was called, on their monthly visits. By kind permission of the present owners I visited the house of my birth recently and was amazed to discover that its current market value was around £187,000. It seems that the neighbourhood has become fashionable as a conservation area and most of the properties have been extensively renovated. In my day, the water supply was confined to the ground floor and was heated on a gas stove. Warmth was provided by coal fires, which were hardly adequate. There was an outside toilet which it was an ordeal to visit in cold weather.

My early childhood was very different from that of children today. Toys were simple and there was not a great choice. I remember having a well-loved teddy bear, but as I grew older so did he, losing first one eye and then the other. His ears were torn, his stuffing began to fall out and at last he had to be thrown away. It was a time of economic depression and there was little money about. As toys were relatively expensive, most children had to make do with home-made ones. My father was quite handy and made me an engine painted bright red, big enough for me to sit in and be pushed along. I also had a wooden horse on wheels which I rode a great deal. When I grew older I was given a small wind-up gramophone complete with few records which I played over and over again until they wore out. I suppose it's not surprising that I still remember some of the tunes. I also had a magic lantern with which I showed coloured slides on a screen, the illumination being provided by a candle firmly fixed inside a metal box with a chimney to allow the heat to escape. I spent many hours playing with my Meccano outfit, with which I built models of cranes, bridges and suchlike. When I played in the street, I used to cover long distances pushing a pram wheel along with a stick. Like most other children, I had a large iron hoop which I trundled along the road, guiding it with a cane. Sometimes I played with a wooden top which had to be whipped with a string fastened to a wooden handle to make it spin. Although these toys were all quite simple, I'm sure they gave us just as much pleasure as the electronic games prevalent today. Radio broadcasts began in the 1920s and "the wireless", as it was called for obvious reasons, became very popular. The receivers (crystal sets) were very simple at first and the reception of programmes depended on the listener's skill in making the right contact between the cat's whisker and the crystal. The cumbersome earphones eventually gave way to loudspeakers, a significant advance. There was, of course, no television at that time.

11

My first few years passed all too quickly and it was time for me to start at the local primary school which was conveniently located close by. The lessons were pretty basic – English, arithmetic, history, geography and a little science. We were also taught singing and country dancing for good measure. Traditional teaching methods were used, and we sat in rows facing the teacher.

There were no group activities at that time. Anniversaries such as Empire Day and Armistice Day were strictly observed. The Oxford and Cambridge boat race was a great occasion and a man selling light blue and dark blue favours at the school gates did a great trade. We exercised in a somewhat inadequate playground, and there was an optional weekly visit to the local swimming baths, but my mother would not allow me to indulge in such a dangerous activity. I was a regular customer at Mrs Grant's sweet shop, strategically located opposite the school. I had a close friend named Bob, whose parents owned the local newsagents, and we shared many enjoyable adventures together. On one occasion he invited me to take a ride in a cart which he had constructed from a plank of wood and a tea chest. It was an ambitious affair with a steering wheel, four rubber-tyred pram wheels, a brake and even a horn. We derived great enjoyment from this contraption, taking turns to push each other down a nearby steep hill. There was little traffic, and by that time we reached the bottom of the hill we were going at a fair speed. It was a long walk back. Once, we pushed our cart as far as the Strand, where we parked it in the kerb and went into Lyons Corner House at Charing Cross for tea. These Corner Houses were very elegant, with tail-coated waiters in place of the usual Nippies. We were about ten years old at that time and not dressed for the occasion. Indeed, I remember that Bob had a rather prominent hole in his trousers. We ordered a pot of tea and some bread and butter, all that we could afford. The waiter who disdainfully served us said sarcastically, "Does your mother know you're out?" He was overheard by an elderly lady at the next table who took him to task for his rudeness. Later I acquired a bicycle which Bob taught me to ride. It became one of my most treasured possessions and I spent many happy days with various friends cycling to destinations within twenty-five miles of London. When war broke out, I decided that I would have no further use for it and sold it for the princely sum of five pounds. Bob and I have remained great friends ever since and telephone each other once a week even now. Our circumstances have improved somewhat since those early days.

I remember very well our family Christmases. Shortly before the great day the folding doors separating the two ground-floor rooms of our house were fastened back, affording us much-needed space. Seasonal decorations abounded, not the ready-made ones now available in great variety but brightly-coloured paper chains laboriously pasted together. The piano was given an extra polish and the extended dining table placed in position. Our oven was stretched to full capacity to accommodate a fifteen-pound turkey with all the trimmings, no frozen birds being available at that time. The whole family – uncles, aunts and cousins – came from all parts of London for the occasion, some twenty strong in all, tightly packed into our small house. My mother was ably assisted by various sisters in serving an excellent meal, after which we settled down to enjoy the rest of the day. My cousins and I retired to an upstairs room, where we played various board games and ate far too many sweets, while the adults below talked incessantly or fell asleep. After tea there was an impromptu concert, with one of my uncles playing the mandolin accompanied on the piano by his daughter. One Christmas, I persuaded everyone, including my grandmother, to sing into a primitive microphone positioned in another room. This simple but effective entertainment caused a good deal of merriment. Much later in the evening it was time for the adults to indulge in a card game called 'Banker'. This lasted until the early hours and a considerable amount of money was wagered. However, an ingenious control system was used whereby nobody could lose or win more than twenty-five pence by the end of the game. Sleeping so many people was a formidable task but it was accomplished, the women and children occupying all the available beds while the men made themselves as comfortable as possible in armchairs or on the floor. Rising late on Boxing Day, we all made our way to South London, where one of my aunts held court. Her children were better educated than me, and I did not feel comfortable playing such intellectual games as charades. However, the time passed pleasantly and we all enjoyed ourselves.

George in 1920

2

The Seaside

Despite our straightened circumstances we spent two weeks at the seaside every year, although how my father saved enough money to pay for this Summer holiday I can't imagine.

Most years, our holiday destination was Ramsgate, some eighty miles away on the north-east Kent coast. More often than not we travelled down from London by paddle-steamer. These vessels operated all through the Summer, except on Fridays when there were no sailings because of a long-standing superstition among sailors that it brought bad luck to put to sea on that day. If I remember rightly, we had a choice of two boats, the "Royal Sovereign" and the "Crested Eagle". We chose the latter because it was the larger and faster, while its departure was at the more civilised hour of nine a.m. We packed our luggage overnight and rose early in the morning, catching a bus to the Monument, close by London Bridge. Then began the long walk to Tower Pier, my father puffing and blowing under the weight of the one suitcase which held the spare clothes and necessities for all three of us. Our route took us through the busy fish market at Billingsgate, which was at that time of the morning crowded with porters pushing heavy barrows and precariously balancing baskets of fish on their heads.

Arriving at last at the pier, in the shadow of the Tower of London, we joined the long queue of people patiently waiting to board the boat. It was a lengthy wait but tolerable – provided the sun was shining, which it usually was. At last the queue began to shuffle forward, to the great excitement of the many children present, and everyone jostled to surge up the gangplank under the watchful eye of the ticket inspector. Once aboard, the first objective was to claim a place on one of the hard and less-than-comfortable wooden seats on deck in the most advantageous position, although if the weather was bad everyone made a beeline for the warmth and comfort of the saloons below. At nine o'clock sharp three loud blasts on the ship's siren signalled our departure and we pulled away from Tower Pier, with the paddle wheels noisily threshing the water, to begin our journey down river, passing between the great bastions of Tower Bridge, raised to allow us through.

This part of the trip never failed to fascinate me as we glided proudly past numerous merchant ships busily unloading the cargoes they had brought from far-away exotic lands. We gazed in wonder at the mighty ocean liners being prepared for their next voyage and marvelled at the great variety of river traffic which could be seen going about its business, fussy tugboats towing obstinate strings of heavy barges cheek by jowl with fishing smacks and colliers. We made our way steadily towards the open sea, stopping briefly at Greenwich and Woolwich to take on more passengers. We passed great factories sprawled on both banks of the river, their tall chimneys belching thick smoke. We could hear the continuous sounds of hammering and the hiss of escaping steam associated with modern manufacturing processes, and occasionally a tiny figure working on a jetty and dwarfed by enormous buildings paused in his labours to give us a friendly wave.

At last we reached the mouth of the Thames and were rewarded with our first glimpse of the mile-long Southend Pier, pointing like a thin finger out to sea. We pulled alongside to disgorge some of our passengers and take on more, then on we went across what I fondly imagined to be the high seas but which was in fact the Thames estuary. With no land in sight, it was time to explore the ship. I made my way first to the entrance of the dining saloon, to stand enveloped in the appetising smells of cooking and to catch a glimpse of the more affluent passengers enjoying their lunch, three courses for the equivalent of 12½ pence. One of my ambitions, never fulfilled, was to eat in that saloon, but we had to be content with sandwiches and a glass of lemonade. I always paid a visit to the engine-room to gaze in rapture at the gleaming machinery steadily pulsating to drive the paddle wheels, while occasionally an overalled engineer deftly applied an oilcan to some vital part. Another place I enjoyed visiting, despite the disapproval of my parents, was the saloon given over to penny-in-the-slot machines which offered the glittering but very slim chance of winning a small fortune. Although my holiday money was strictly limited (25 pence in all) I could never resist feeding a few coins into these machines, usually losing the lot in the end after a few false triumphs.

We felt that our holiday had really begun when Margate pier loomed out of the distance. Pulling alongside our pierhead berth we could see the sandy beaches packed with people reclining in deck chairs or splashing around in the water. In the background was the long promenade and the entrance to the Dreamland funfair. There were times when, because of strong winds and rough seas, we had to disembark at Margate and continue our journey to Ramsgate by electric tram, something of an anti-climax. Usually, however, we were able to complete our voyage by sea. On arrival at Ramsgate our boat was met by numerous small boys with handcarts offering to transport our luggage from the pierhead to the town. My father sternly rejected their approaches, determined to carry the luggage himself, whatever the discomfort and distance involved.

My father booked bed-and-breakfast accommodation some months in advance, selecting one of the many establishments advertising in a publication called Dalton's Weekly. It cost the equivalent of about 62½ pence per person per week. For that sort of money we could hardly expect anything lavish and inevitably our lodgings were situated a very long way from the seafront. A jug of cold water and a basin were provided for our ablutions, although my father would be allowed the luxury of a mug of hot water for shaving. If we were lucky there was an indoor toilet, usually some way from the bedroom, but of course no bathroom. The lack of a bath was no deprivation, since at home we bathed only once every three weeks because of the difficulties and expense of heating sufficient water in the stone copper and carrying it by the pailful to a tin bath in front of the kitchen fire. The breakfast was generally adequate but the standard of cleanliness sometimes left a lot to be desired. I remember one morning being unable to open my eyes when I awoke because my eyelids were swollen with bites from bed-bugs, a common enough pest in those days. My father was an ultra-cautious man and it was his custom to pay the landlady in full for our accommodation immediately we arrived. He felt that this was a safeguard in case he should subsequently lose his wallet. The drawback was that once he had paid over the money his

Ramsgate in the twenties

18

bargaining power was that much weaker should he have cause to complain about the standard of the food or the accommodation. We ate our mid-day dinner and early evening meal at a large Lyons restaurant just off the seafront. My father fancied himself as something of a wit and would exchange light-hearted pleasantries with the waitresses – there was no self-service in those days. He made a great play of handing out what was to him a lavish tip after the meal, much to the embarrassment of my mother and me.

Our days followed much the same pattern. My father rose early and went off for a solitary walk, in the course of which he bought his newspaper. After breakfast we made our way slowly through the busy streets to the seafront where we hired deckchairs and staked our claim to a few square feet of sandy beach. By mid-morning the main sands were crowded and latecomers had difficulty in finding a space. My father buried himself in his newspaper, occasionally emerging to take a walk along by the harbour, while my mother was content to bask in the sun. I played with my bucket and spade, building and demolishing sandcastles as my mood dictated. I remember once taking part in a sandcastle competition. I would have won a prize too, but for the intervention of a jealous parent who told the judges that my father had helped me, strictly against the rules of the competition of course. The beach had its own variety of entertainments. Twice each day there was a Punch and Judy show, weather permitting, and scores of children sat in untidy rows on the sand engrossed in watching the age-old story unfold with all its humour and violence. Their excitement reached a crescendo when they screamed out warnings to Mr Punch to look out for the voracious crocodile. While the show was in progress a man circulated hopefully among the crowds with a canvas bag, collecting coppers from the appreciative audience. A dozen or so sad-eyed donkeys, their names emblazoned on their leather headbands, paraded on the sands when the tide was right and waited patiently to give brief and bumpy rides to queues of eager youngsters, many of whom had very little contact with live animals except on such occasions. Sometimes, greatly daring, we paddled in the sea. All three of us were non-swimmers and didn't possess a bathing costume between us. In fact, my father's sole concession to the holiday spirit was to wear white tennis shoes with shiny black toe caps in place of his usual tightly-laced black boots.

After lunch we forsook the delights of the beach and sought adventure further afield. In the earlier years we took a ride in a horse-brake, a ponderous, creaking, four-wheeled conveyance carrying some twelve people sitting in rows on hard wooden benches. It was usually drawn by two long-suffering animals, but when steep hills were encountered, as at the Royal Parade, a third horse was called in to help take the strain. The journeys all started from Ramsgate harbour, and one favourite destination was the lavender fields at Minster (still in existence, I believe), where my mother always bought a small bottle of the fragrant perfume. Another journey took us to the then tiny village of Birchington, which I hated because it seemed so dreary and desolate. Little did I dream that much later in life I would spend many enjoyable years of retirement in that same village.

In the course of time the horse-brakes were replaced by motor-coaches or "charabancs" as they were called. These were, of course, able to cover much greater distances than the horses, and the whole of East Kent was thus within easy reach. The coaches lined up at Ramsgate harbour every morning, afternoon and evening, displaying boards listing their various destinations and the prices. Hoarse-voiced salesmen vied with one another to sell seats and it was all highly competitive. To secure a place for the more popular excursions it was necessary to get to the coaches long before the appointed departure time, and I well recall sitting uncomfortably for what seemed hours on an unbearably hot coach seat exposed to the blazing sun, impatiently waiting for the journey to begin. As well as fine days there were, of course, wet days, when the drivers would struggle to pull into position the heavy canvas awnings which provided some degree of protection for the unfortunate passengers.

Every year we took a trip to Canterbury, where we reverently toured the awe-inspiring cathedral and visited the ancient weavers' cottages overhanging the river. We took refreshments in one of the very many delightful tearooms staffed by well-bred ladies who somehow made us feel that they were doing us a favour by condescending to serve us. Never mind, their teas were delicious if somewhat expensive.

20

On some occasions we took a full-day drive, first to Dover where we enjoyed an hour's coffee break, then on to Folkestone for lunch, returning to Ramsgate in time for tea. This provided a great day's entertainment for a very modest outlay, even allowing for the driver's tip. The Mystery Tour was another favourite excursion although more often than not the destination turned out to be somewhere quite ordinary and not exciting at all.

We made full use of the cheap and frequent electric trams to visit nearer attractions. We always made a trip to Broadstairs to be entertained by the famous Uncle Mac and his Minstrels at the end of the jetty. With their blackened faces, banjos and plantation songs they were highly popular, although these days I suppose they would be considered racist. We spent another full day visiting Margate, which was always considered somewhat vulgar and inferior to Ramsgate. However, it had some attractive aspects, the best of which I suppose was Dreamland. Admission was free and it was always packed with holidaymakers, mostly day trippers from London, some riding on the several gaily-painted roundabouts or enjoying a thrill on the Big Dipper, others contenting themselves with viewing the many side shows and crowding round the stalls packed with what seemed to me glittering prizes but which were in reality shoddy merchandise, no doubt.

My father usually took himself off one evening to visit "the dogs", the greyhound racing stadium at Dumpton. Although he was not a gambling man (in fact, the very opposite) this was the one annual occasion on which he threw caution to the winds. He never revealed how much he staked nor the extent of his winnings, or losings, but always claimed to break even. When he went off on this harmless jaunt my mother and I spent the evening at one of the several cinemas vying for our custom. In those days it was the practice for the very latest films to be released to the seaside resorts during the peak holiday season, and I vividly remember being scared out of my wits watching the original version of "King Kong" with its revolutionary special effects. This was, of course, before the advent of television, when cinemas were packed to the doors and long queues were the order of the day.

We spent at least one evening each week being entertained by Harry Gold's concert party. Since Ramsgate did not boast a pier as such, the performances took place on a wooden stage built right on the sands near the harbour. The most expensive seats consisted of several rows of deck chairs at the front of the fenced enclosure, but we usually occupied the cheaper hard wooden forms further back from the stage. The price of admission was about three pence (1¼p) but this was doubled on so-called "gala" nights. There were about eight performers, four of each sex, made up of a compère, comedian, magician, pianist and assorted singers. They all worked very hard, relying heavily on audience participation, and in general they presented very acceptable, if unsophisticated, entertainment. Another somewhat superior concert party performed, on Sunday evenings only, in a theatre on the East Cliff. I always thought this a very dull affair, especially as – to comply with the law – the artistes appeared in evening dress, no make-up or fancy dress being allowed on the Sabbath. Although the cinemas were open on Sunday evenings, none of our family would dream of seeing a film on that day, since in our circles it was thought not quite the proper thing to do. When at home we attended church several times every Sunday but when on holiday the only religious building we ever entered was Canterbury Cathedral, and that was just for the purpose of sightseeing.

Not content with travelling between London and Ramsgate by sea, we made at least one local boat trip during our holiday. I will never forget a rugged sailing ship called the "Moss Rose" which made what were laughingly called "pleasure" trips at regular intervals. On one occasion we set sail from Ramsgate harbour on this vessel in brilliant sunshine, but within a very short space of time strong gale-force winds blew up from nowhere. Thus our projected short sea cruise was prolonged by several hours as we struggled to return to the calm waters of the harbour. The seasoned crew members, who had seen it all before, were kept busy cleaning up after the many seasick passengers, of which I was one. I should have known better than to have blackberry and apple pie for lunch before leaving the safety of the land. As the years passed, sailing vessels gave way to motor-launches, which certainly seemed more stable if not so picturesque. Later still, speedboat trips were all the rage, despite their brevity and horrendous expense, all of 25p a time.

Safely back on land, some of our time was spent playing endless games of putting on the still-existing greens on the West Cliff. I always won, but with hindsight I suspect that this was not because of my superior skill but because my parents did not want to spoil my evident delight in victory – I was not a good loser. Tiring of such strenuous activity, we strolled to the cliff edge to admire the elaborate pictures of cathedrals and castles being drawn in the sand far below. People tossed pennies to the artist, who gathered them before the relentless tide advanced and destroyed his handiwork. On hot days we took refuge in the pleasant greenery of nearby Ellington Park, where we lazed in deckchairs or sat on the grass enjoying one of the many band concerts which took place there. On occasions there were talent contests which caused a great deal of amusement, sometimes to the discomfort of the competitors.

My mother was greatly intrigued by what the future might hold and always found time to visit a fortune teller. She never disclosed what she was told but usually seemed to derive some satisfaction from her briefing. Once she had my head examined by a phrenologist but, as far as I remember, nothing he forecast about my future ever came to pass. Occasionally I tried my hand at fishing from the harbour wall with a handline but, to my great disgust, I never caught anything other than crabs.

The first week of the holiday seemed to pass very slowly but the second one flashed past at the speed of lightning. No sooner had Monday evening gone than it was Saturday morning, our last day at the seaside. It was time to return home to the reality of life in London. Most of our packing had been done overnight, since we were expected to vacate our lodgings immediately after breakfast, come rain or shine. As the paddle steamer was not due to leave until late afternoon, we spent the last few hours sadly wandering round the town buying the obligatory last-minute gifts of brightly-coloured and lettered seaside rock for those unfortunates left at home. I'm not quite sure what happened to our luggage but I have a vague recollection of my father handing it into a store for safekeeping until it was time to board the boat.

As the time for departure approached, a straggly procession of weary souls plodded up the gangplank, but this time the objective of the more experienced travellers was to find a seat not on deck but in one of the cabins below, for although we took our holidays in August the homeward voyage could be a distinctly chilly experience, particularly after darkness fell. It could also be quite boring, certainly until after we had reached Southend. Then began our slow progress up-river towards London. Traffic on the river was minimal and there was little visible activity on its banks, the factories having closed down for the weekend. Because of the width of the "Crested Eagle" and the narrowness of the Thames above Tower Bridge, it was necessary for the boat to turn face about at Greenwich and travel backwards for the remaining few miles of the journey to ensure that it was properly positioned for its departure from Tower Pier the following morning. This, of course, meant that its speed was considerably reduced, especially if a strong adverse tide was running, and it was sometimes almost midnight before we were able to disembark. Once ashore, it was a case of making our way as fast as possible to London Bridge in the hope that we could catch a late night bus home.

For the first few days after our return I felt as if I was living in a different world, but soon memories of the holiday would fade like a dream and it was back to reality for another twelve months.

3

The Church

Apart from my father, who was only an occasional church-goer, my family were deeply religious, and as soon as I was old enough I was introduced to the Sunday school at the nearby St. Peter's church. One of my aunts played the piano for this gathering and I was installed in a chair on the platform after refusing to sit with the other children, such was my lack of self-confidence. In due course I joined the Cubs and then graduated to the choir. Later, I became a server and even later a teacher at the Sunday school. The organist and choirmaster was a somewhat pompous but well-meaning man who held choir practice every Friday evening and played the organ at both morning and evening services on Sunday. He must have enjoyed his work, since he lived quite a long way from the church and earned a mere pittance. His playing left a lot to be desired and his attempted rendering of Widor's Toccata, one of his favourite pieces, was never entirely successful, but at least he attended regularly.

During most of my adolescence I attended church four times every Sunday, but I must confess that this was not entirely because I was devoutly religious. At the tender age of thirteen I fell madly in love with a girl named Dorothy, whom I was eventually to marry, and the church made a convenient meeting place. My good friend Arthur, a fellow choirboy with an excellent tenor voice, was not so fortunate in love. He worshipped from afar a pretty girl from an upper-class family who was well aware of his devotion but did nothing to encourage him. We used to talk endlessly about a strategy to improve their relationship but all to no avail. The girl eventually married a World War 2 fighter pilot who sadly was killed soon afterwards. Arthur called on me some years later when I was living in Streatham, bringing with him his fiancee, a shy young lady who hardly had a word to say. My friend, too, was not forthcoming and did not suggest a further meeting. I have not heard from him since and do not know whether he is married or single, dead or alive.

The Vicar was a handsome man who suffered from shell shock, which caused him to have an unfortunate speech impediment, a great drawback to someone in his position. We got on very well, and at the age of sixteen I was allowed to edit the parish magazine, which had a circulation of no less than a hundred and fifty. Dorothy's best friend was a very attractive girl and caused a scandal by marrying the Vicar, who was some thirty years older than her, soon after the outbreak of war. Despite all the dire prophecies of the congregation, the marriage was a long and happy one, blessed by two children. The Vicar lived until the age of ninety, although sadly his widow died in her late sixties.

There were, of course, many social activities promoted by the church. Every year there was a Christmas party for the Sunday school children, each of whom received an attractive present from Father Christmas, although there was precious little money available. They ate jam sandwiches and cakes, washed down with lemonade, and the church hall resounded with their laughter. In the Summer there was an outing to Chingford in the nearby countryside. On the appointed day the children assembled at the church and marched to the railway station, where they were loaded onto the train under the supervision of the teachers and helpers. After a picnic lunch the afternoon was spent in enjoying all the fun of the fair. Once tea was over, the children were shepherded back to the station for the homeward journey.

The church had a dramatic society which regularly presented various shows at the church hall. On one memorable occasion my father, normally a shy and reticent man, was persuaded to take a minor part in a play called "Tilly of Bloomsbury" and acquitted himself well, much to my mother's surprise. Every November a bazaar took place, spread over a Friday evening and Saturday afternoon and evening. A great deal of hard work went into this event, which usually raised not far short of a hundred pounds, a great deal of money in those days. When I was just fifteen I began organising dances in aid of church funds. These took place at the church hall and became very popular, attracting an attendance of around two hundred. The hire of an excellent dance band, playing for a full three hours, cost just over three pounds, plus refreshments. Taking place in our somewhat rough neighbourhood, the dances inevitably attracted an undesirable element, but I always took the precaution of bribing the local policeman to put in an appearance from time to time. There were occasional children's dancing displays, and sometimes rather more formal concerts featuring singers and musicians. One of my aunts used to sing at these concerts, but although she had a very fine voice she lacked the finance to be properly trained. Now in her nineties, she can still sing a few high notes and tinkle away at the piano.

Shortly after meeting Dorothy for the first time, I was given two tickets for Bertram Mills Circus at the Olympia. Greatly daring, I called to see her mother and asked permission to take Dorothy to this event. Visibly shaken, she said she would talk to her daughter and let me know what she decided. The next day, Dorothy called at my house and told my mother she could not accept my invitation as she was attending evening classes. I discovered later that this was just an excuse. My mother was horrified at my audacity in issuing this invitation to a girl she didn't know. At the earliest opportunity she apologised to Dorothy's mother, and this led to a deep friendship which lasted for the rest of their lives. Undaunted, I took every opportunity to see my new love. I discovered that she took her dog for a walk most evenings and often managed to waylay her. Her poor dog found itself suffering from a surfeit of exercise, which did it no harm since it was grossly overweight. We also used to meet frequently at the library, causing Dorothy's mother to be surprised at her daughter's sudden interest in books. I even used to waylay her on her way to work and again on her way home in the evenings. In short, I became a real pest, but my persistence paid off and we became inseparable. Although Dorothy was working at a Court dressmakers in the West End, I was still at grammar school and had very little money to spend on courtship. Fortunately, there was no shortage of cheap entertainment. Clissold Park, with its boating lake, aviary and animals (including deer, kangaroos, guinea pigs and rabbits) was within walking distance. We spent many hours there under the benevolent eye of the uniformed park attendant, who maintained order with little problem. In the Summer there were band concerts, and tennis courts were available for the more energetic. The 1930s were the days of the super cinemas, where a four-hour programme of two full-length films, stage show, organ recital, newsreel and cartoons,

Teenagers George and Dorothy

cost the equivalent of just 2½ pence. Performances were continuous from lunchtime onwards and long queues were the order of the day. Some West End theatres, which were finding it difficult to compete with the cinemas, issued privilege tickets offering a fifty per cent discount on the price, and we took full advantage of this concession. Transport was cheap and plentiful, and a day out at the seaside or in the country was within the reach of most people. There were plenty of open-air public swimming baths to be enjoyed in Summer, while there was a wealth of pantomimes and circuses around Christmas. Local variety theatres, with famous names topping the bill, struggled to survive and offered great value for money. With the advent of television that state of affairs changed, but theatres are still holding their own and cinemas have enjoyed a revival in recent years.

In 1937 my romance was dealt what I thought at the time to be a mortal blow. Dorothy's father was appointed resident engineer at Kings College Hospital in Camberwell, south-east London. I thought that this physical separation would mean the end of our friendship, and the bottom was about to drop out of my world. However, I need not have worried. Our respective parents were very understanding and agreed to our spending alternate week-ends together at Dalston and Camberwell. I might add that there was no question of our sharing a bedroom, and in fact we didn't have much time to be alone.

4

One Man's War

When I first went to school I hated it, and there were occasions when my long-suffering mother had great difficulty in dragging me there. Fortunately for me, however, one of the teachers was a source of great encouragement, and with her help I won a Junior County Scholarship at the age of eleven. Travelling to Westminster City School, where I was to spend the next seven years, entailed a train and bus journey across London, and this helped me to become more self-reliant. At the age of fourteen I acquired a bicycle and cycled to school, an easy journey at that time but not one I would like to attempt now.

The headmaster, a small man but well-built, could strike fear into the hearts of miscreants with one glance. The teachers, all male with one exception, "Lizzie", who taught English and religious knowledge to the youngest pupils, were held in great respect. Most of them had been at the school long before I joined and were still there when I left. They wore their gowns with pride, and one of them, affectionately nicknamed "Oily", a Jewish gentleman with an imposing presence, even wore a mortar-board. Most of the pupils were scholarship boys, although there were a few fee-payers. On the whole, I enjoyed my time there and managed to cope with my studies quite well. I was never keen on sport but took part in various activities, joining the dramatic society and appearing in several productions, even playing the villain on one occasion. The school concerts were eagerly awaited, and some of the more courageous masters often took part. I remember the deputy head giving a spirited rendering of "Drake's Drum" at every possible opportunity. The school orchestra was conducted by a diminutive master who taught maths to the older boys. After prophesying that we would all end up as dustmen, he explained that we could avoid this degradation by attending his after-school classes in maths, for which he charged five shillings per term. Most of us took advantage of his offer, fearful of the consequences if we declined. Every day began with an assembly which included prayers, bible reading, a hymn and various announcements. The commanding officer of our army cadet force was named Captain Shackle, and we delighted in singing with great vigour a hymn which included the words "Then shall all shackles fall, the stormy clangor of wild war music over all the earth shall cease".

The school was, and still is, located in Palace Street, Westminster, opposite what was then Whitbreads brewery. At times the sweet stench of hops was overpowering and noisy horse-drawn drays clattered into the loading bays. It was only a few minutes' walk to St. James's park, where I spent many a lunch-hour walking round the lake or visiting the London Museum (now Lancaster House). Discipline was maintained by prefects drawn from the sixth form. Conduct marks were given to those boys foolish enough to misbehave, and those who acquired three or more during a week suffered detention. We enjoyed an excellent all-round education and our success rate in the Oxford School Certificate and the Higher School Certificate was proof of this. Having passed the former exam with honours, I had hopes of going on to the university with the intention of eventually teaching classics. Regretfully, I failed the Higher School Certificate in just one of the four subjects required. In view of my parents' humble circumstances, I could not afford to wait another year to re-take the examination, so I was faced with the prospect of finding a job, a task no easier in those days than it is now. I registered with an organisation called the Headmasters Employment Bureau, and in due course presented myself for various interviews. The first was with a firm of stockbrokers called Kitkat and Aitken (still in existence today under a somewhat different name) but I failed to pass their arithmetic test. Next I was offered a job with the newly-formed Air Raid Precautions Department of a local authority (this was in 1938) but I declined as it was only temporary.

My third interview was with the New Zealand High Commission in London, where I was offered a job, again temporary, as a cadet, a sort of general dogsbody. I accepted – and stayed for the next forty years. Of course, New Zealanders occupied the top jobs, but most of the staff were locally recruited. I met some really great characters at New Zealand

House, among them Bill Jordan, who was High Commissioner at that time. A true Cockney and an astute politician, he was universally popular and a favourite with the Royal Family. He had started his working life as a policeman, and he was fond of saying that he began as P.C. Jordan and finished up as Jordan, P.C. (Privy Councillor). The mixture of New Zealanders and English staff worked well, and I enjoyed some happy times at New Zealand House.

Sadly, this state of affairs was not to last, as the threat of war loomed nearer. Our chief clerk was intensely patriotic and insisted that we cadets enlisted in the Territorial Army. I was very reluctant but did not want to jeopardise my career and so I joined the Queen's Westminster Rifles. Almost immediately I was instructed to attend a Summer camp at Beaulieu in Hampshire. I asked the chief clerk if he could get me excused, saying how inconvenient it would be for the office for me to be away so soon after joining the staff. He dismissed my suggestion and granted me extra leave of absence. Thus it was that I came to endure a miserable week in camp, spending most of my time drilling or washing up countless greasy tin plates in tepid water. My tent, which I shared with some seven others, was close to the camp cinema, where a noisy Crazy Gang film called "O.K. for Sound" was screened three times daily. I got to know the soundtrack by heart.

In September of the following year war broke out. Being a Territorial I was called up immediately and reported to my Regimental Headquarters in Westminster. We were loaded into an Underground train and transported to a school in Harrow Road. Unfortunately it was an infants' school and all the toilet facilities were scaled down accordingly, causing some of my heftier colleagues considerable difficulty in performing their ablutions. It is not generally known that I was the first casualty of the war. Some idiot had leaned his rifle against the wall, and during the first night it crashed down on to my head, cutting it open. You can imagine the comments when I appeared next morning, heavily bandaged. I later found out that it was *my* rifle that had caused the damage. I found myself posted to the headquarters of the 1st London Division. The method of assigning us to our duties was not too scientific. Someone who was a butcher in civilian life would be made a latrine attendant, a carpenter

33

would become a cook, and so on. Any men left over whom they could not place were assigned to the Intelligence. With my clerical experience I was the obvious choice as batman to the G.O.C. Fortunately, he was a very kind and tolerant man and I spent the next three years comparatively happily with him in various locations in the south of England. In addition to looking after the General, I worked in the officers' mess and waited at table on many distinguished guests, including the Duke of Gloucester, General "Jumbo" Wilson, and the Archbishop of Canterbury.

Then the powers-that-be decided that our Division should go overseas. Regretfully, the General was too old for active service and he was sent off to form the RAF Regiment, while I was promoted to take charge of the officers' mess. I did my best to avoid going overseas by developing a severe attack of tonsillitis, which resulted in my tonsils being removed in Colchester Military Hospital where they served toast for breakfast on the morning following the operation. My efforts were of no avail, however, and in September 1942 we set sail from Liverpool. Now, I'm not a good sailor and the next few weeks on the troopship were distinctly uncomfortable, to say the least. It did not help when, as an acting corporal, I was appointed guard commander on one occasion to keep an eye on two unfortunate prisoners in the cells. When Company Orders were posted next morning I was horrified to see that I had been placed on a charge. It seemed that when the Camp Commandant was doing his rounds he had found a cigarette butt in one of the cells. Fortunately, I was able to argue that the NCO who had relieved me had signed the book to say that everything was in order when he took over, thus the cigarette butt could not possibly have been there when I was on duty. The Camp Commandant was convinced, quite rightly, that I was guilty, but he had no choice but to dismiss the charge on a technicality. The rest of the voyage was uneventful and we sailed safely, first to Cape Town and thence to Bombay, where we were transferred to a French ship in which the toilet facilities were so appalling that I developed constipation which lasted a full week.

At last we reached Basra in the Persian Gulf and were transported in primitive and uncomfortable wooden railway carriages through Iraq to Kirkuk, where the oilfields were situated. This part of Iraq is sometimes called the end of the world, and rightly so. The only entertainment for the troops was a primitive cinema run by the locals. For the most part, the films shown were in poor condition, the actors and actresses almost unrecognisable and the dialogue unintelligible. However, on one occasion everything was going well. The picture was clear, the sound good and the subject enthralling. Unfortunately, as the climax was approaching, the projector broke down. The lights went up and the troops waited patiently for some minutes for the programme to continue. But it didn't continue, and to everyone's fury the strains of the National Anthem came over the loudspeakers. The audience was furious and gave vent to their feelings by completely wrecking the place. After that, we did not even have a cinema.

Our misery did not last much longer, however, and we were soon on our way by road through Syria, Palestine (as it was then known) and Egypt to join the 8th Army in the desert. The battle of El Alamein had been fought and won and we advanced in to Tunisia with little opposition. So far, I hadn't seen any action, and I was quite happy about that, but things were soon to change. We set up camp at a place called Enfidaville at the foot of a range of mountains where the enemy was entrenched. Our G.O.C. had decided that we would be quite safe on the open plain, but very soon we were being shelled, not a pleasant experience. Ironically, the first shell hit the command caravan, wounding the General in the head and effectively putting him out of the war. I had suspected his judgement back in Iraq when, against all advice, he had ordered camp to be pitched in a wadi (or valley), which was turned into a turbulent river overnight by torrential rain. The war was getting too close for comfort, in addition to which the officers were still insisting on maintaining standards which they had enjoyed in England, although conditions were far from ideal and hygiene was a problem in the mess. One day, General Montgomery came to lunch. He was small in stature but very positive in manner, and made it quite clear that he did not approve of drinking and smoking. He used to issue printed leaflets telling us what was happening in the field of battle and what he was going to do next. Nobody read them, of course, but as they were roughly the same size as a sheet of toilet paper they were put to good use.

While I was with the 8th Army, a call went out for volunteers to join the Field Security Service, a branch of the Intelligence Corps. Forgetting the age-old maxim, "Never Volunteer", I put my name forward. I had no worthwhile qualifications except a grammar school education and a smattering of schoolboy French, but they must have been desperate for volunteers and I was accepted. I was packed off to the Intelligence Corps training depot at Helwan, a pleasant suburb of Cairo, where I started a course of instruction. Because of the Official Secrets Act I cannot give precise details of my training, but I can tell you that it included instruction on how to ride a motor-bike. Most of my fellow-trainees were ex-schoolteachers, which was understandable because of their high level of intelligence and their knowledge of foreign languages. Regretfully, they were not very practical, and mastering the art of riding a motor-bike proved very difficult for some of them. Part of our training was to ride up a sandhill at full speed as far as we could, turn round and ride down again without stalling the engine or falling off the machine. It was a hilarious sight. Sand, of course, was the main problem – it got everywhere. One unfortunate once found that his throttle had jammed in the open position. Manfully, he pushed his bike through deep sand which suddenly thinned out, causing the machine to shoot off at high speed, with the rider clinging desperately to the handlebars. Our numbers included a Frenchman who claimed to be bi-lingual, but whose knowledge of the English vernacular left a lot to be desired. Once, during motor-bike training, the instructor said "Now, when I give the word, I want you to start up your bikes. Ready? Kick 'em over". The next moment the Frenchman's bike was lying on the ground while he stood by with a puzzled look on his face – he had taken the command rather too literally.

When my training was complete I was posted to a Field Security Section in a place called Baalbek in the Lebanon. This was the site of some famous ruins, but we didn't appreciate their importance at that time. They were guarded (for want of a better word) by East African troops who were ill-equipped for the severe Winter weather. On more than one occasion, these unfortunates were found literally frozen stiff at their posts, and had to be carried back to the guardroom to be thawed out. Some of the locals were expert thieves. They used to strip off naked and smother their bodies with grease. On the rare occasions when they were discovered raiding an encampment it was almost impossible to get a grip on them and very few were caught. One of my jobs was to liaise with an informant called Sheik Amin. He was a civil servant and used to keep me informed of the many rumours which were constantly circulating. I was a sergeant at that time, but he was convinced that, in reality, I was at least a colonel – would that it were true. There were some Australian troops in our district with some enterprising characters among their numbers. Rumour had it that one patrol used to set up a road block where they would sell rifles to unsuspecting locals. Once they had made a sale, they would telephone a collaborating patrol further along the road, who would stop the natives and confiscate the guns which they knew they were carrying. A very lucrative pastime while it lasted.

After some months in the Lebanon I was posted to Algiers, where I was involved in port security. The invasion of Italy had taken place, and once I had satisfied myself that the action had moved sufficiently far north I managed to arrange a transfer to Brindisi, a small port on the Adriatic coast of southern Italy. By this time I had become an expert in port security and I was allocated a launch, complete with two Italian sailors. My job was to visit ships anchoring just off Brindisi and check on any new crew members and the like. My favourite customers were the many Liberty ships. I used to plan my visits to these ships to take place just before mid-day, when the American crews ate. Invariably, I was invited to lunch on board. The variety and standard of food on those ships had to be seen to be believed. But the Americans were always short of Scotch. As a sergeant, I had a monthly allocation of spirits, and when I went on board a Liberty ship I always took at least one bottle with me. This was traded for 7lb tins of fruit salad, fresh meat and other luxuries we wanted for the mess. Later, I was transferred to Naples, still on port security, but it was less exciting there. However, on one occasion I was assigned to be personal bodyguard to a Yugoslav colonel who was in danger because of his Royalist sympathies, since Tito was now in control of the country. We spent a very pleasant two weeks in a rest camp in Salerno, enjoying the best of food and occupying the best seats at the various entertainments laid on. It was then decided that the colonel would be safer in America and I went with him to the airport where, sadly, I discovered that I was to be left behind in Italy. What I would have done had the colonel been attacked while I was supposed to be guarding him, I don't know.

The Field Security section to which I belonged was then ordered to Austria. This involved travelling up through Italy by motorbike, stopping for a few days at such places of interest as Rome and Florence. We had one amusing incident en route. In one town we stored our motorbikes overnight in a glass-fronted shop. One of my impractical teacher colleagues decided to clean the sparking plug on his bike. He had a vague idea of what to do. He removed the plug, filled a tin lid with petrol and carefully carried it across the wooden shop floor, well away from the motorbikes, intending to lay the plug in the tin lid and set light to the petrol. Unfortunately, he had filled the tin lid to overflowing, and when he lit a match the spilt petrol was ignited. The flames shot across the floor and his bike was set on fire. They managed to save the other machines and the shop but, of course, he was put on a charge. He had to pay the cost of a new motorbike, estimated in those days at just £10.

We eventually reached Austria and I spent the rest of my time in the Army in a little mountain village called Murau, not far from Klagenfurt. Our detachment was allocated a very comfortable detached house, complete with a civilian cook, two housemaids and a handyman to look after our transport. There wasn't a lot to do. I made one unsuccessful attempt at horseriding, but the horse soon realised who was in control and, after ambling gently along for a short while, he turned round and went back to the stables, despite my efforts to steer him in the other direction. Occasionally, an informant would give us details of an ex-enemy officer hiding out in the area and we would set out to find him. We would call on the suspect and the conversation would go something like this: "Excuse me, are you Herr Schmidt, by any chance?" "Yes, I am." "Were you an Ortsgruppenfuhrer?" "Yes, as a matter of fact, I was." "Ah, in that case, perhaps you would be good enough to come with us to the police station." It was all very civilised.

I never stop asking myself how on earth we won the war, faced with the might and efficiency of the Germans and Japanese. I suppose it's because we are experts in improvisation or, more exactly, "muddling through". Believe me, no-one is better in that field than our Intelligence services.

5

Marriage and Suburbia

Soon after the outbreak of war, I asked Dorothy to marry me, and to my delight she accepted. We envisaged a long engagement, but in the Summer of 1940 it was rumoured that my Division was to go overseas. We decided to bring forward our wedding and were married at St. Peter's Church on 21 December 1940. The announcement of the wedding date to my army comrades gave rise to some ribald comments. Until then, I had not realised that 21 December was the longest night of the year. We had arranged to spend our brief honeymoon in Whipsnade at a sub-post office and general store which took paying guests. We arrived there early in the evening, and our hostess, an excellent cook, served a delicious meal. I sometimes tease my Wife by declaring that the only thing I remember about our wedding night was the salmon fishcakes. Our bedroom was icy cold, with just one candle for light, and there was no bathroom, just a chemical toilet. We had stayed up later than expected and it was almost nine-thirty when we went to bed. We could hear the lions at the nearby zoo roaring, but for some reason this did not disturb us too much. We were reminded that there was a war on the next evening, when the bus on which we were returning home burst into flames in the blackout, and we made haste to distance ourselves from it in case any enemy bombers were lurking overhead.

In the event, I did not go overseas until September 1942, so Dorothy and I were able to spend some fragmented time together. As soon as the air raids on London began, Dorothy's father forbade her to continue working in the West End. As a married woman, Dorothy was not immediately liable to be drafted into the Services, and she was given the task of making uniforms for the nurses at Kings College Hospital, where she was living with her father, the resident engineer. Life was difficult for her, as conditions at the hospital were understandably chaotic at times. Whenever an air raid warning sounded, the children had to be taken from

Wartime wedding

40

their wards to the basement, where they were marginally safer. Every available worker had to play a part in coping with the fire-bombs, which landed on the hospital roof with monotonous regularity at the height of the blitz. Ironically, living in London, my Wife was in far greater danger than I was; despite my extensive service overseas, I saw precious little action.

My long-awaited discharge from the Army came in February 1946. There was great jubilation when my Wife and I were re-united after more than three years, but the sense of euphoria did not last for long. Within days, I reported back to the New Zealand High Commission to resume my position as a junior clerk. I must say that my employers treated us ex-servicemen very generously. They had paid our superannuation dues throughout the war and had made up our pitifully small service pay to that of our equivalent rank in the New Zealand Army. In addition, they gave our wives an allowance and gave us an additional end-of-war gratuity. Throughout the war, we had received notional salary increases, and I was highly delighted to be told that my new wage would be seven pounds a week, a considerable increase on my Army pay.

During my overseas service I had managed to save a few hundred pounds as I neither drank or smoked, and Dorothy had put to one side her marriage allowance. Consequently, we decided that we could now afford to buy a house. We were not the only ones looking for accommodation, and finding a suitable property was not easy. By a stroke of luck we made contact with a local firm which was about to build a small number of semi-detached houses in Streatham, south-west London. The price of new properties was strictly controlled in the early post-war years, and in London the ceiling was set at a mere £1,300. We immediately put down a deposit and awaited developments. It was a long wait, since there were many unforseen delays in the construction of the houses, but we did not dare to ask for the return of our deposit for fear that we would not get another similar opportunity. To add to our problems, Dorothy was expecting our first baby. We had made a deliberate decision not to have children until the war had ended. When we decided we could go ahead, it was not as easy as we had thought, and conception took some time. However, it was fun trying. Our daughter Jennifer was born in January 1947, and we had to continue living with

Dorothy's parents until the following November, when the house was ready for occupation. Before we moved, Jennifer was christened in King's College Hospital Chapel, a great event witnessed by some thirty relatives and friends.

Some eighteen months had passed since we took the first steps towards buying the house, and we could hardly believe that the time had come for us to move in. We had visited the site at frequent intervals to watch it being built, and we enjoyed a celibratory dinner when the chimney pots were, at last, put in position. However, this celebration proved to be somewhat premature, and it was not until 21 November 1947 (Princess Elizabeth's wedding day) that we took possession. It was a very cold and damp day, but all went well and by late afternoon we were installed, surrounded by all our worldly possessions. Our first night was uneventful. Jennifer had been left in the care of her grandparents so we were able to give our full attention to getting the essentials unpacked and put into place. On the next day (Saturday), a calamity occurred. The builders had not turned on the water supply but had left us a turncock to operate the stopcock when we needed it. Late that afternoon, I went to turn on the stopcock, which was located in the pavement outside the front gate. Having turned on the water, I tugged at the turncock to release it, but it would not move. I applied more pressure and, suddenly, a column of water shot into the air. Horrified at this development, I rushed to telephone the water board. In a surprisingly short time, two workmen arrived and proceeded to dig up the pavement to stop the leak. They were followed by a stern-faced official who gave me a lecture on the folly of tampering with the water mains. I apologised profusely, expecting to receive a hefty bill from the water board, but in the event I heard nothing further.

It did not take us long to settle in and we were soon re-united with our nine-month-old daughter, who was to enjoy having her own bedroom for the first time. She was a very light sleeper and had shared our bedroom since birth. I don't recall having one undisturbed night during that time, but now that she had her own room she slept like a log, and so did we. So began our introduction to suburban life, and very pleasant it was, too. Streatham was a considerable improvement on our previous neighbourhoods. It was ideally located in relation to my office in the Strand, a journey of about forty minutes by bus and train. It was a good shopping centre and there was ample entertainment provided by a large theatre, an ice rink, a swimming pool, two cinemas and even a night-club for the more sophisticated, while Streatham Common was within easy walking distance. Our new neighbours were friendly and there was a church just a hundred yards away to meet our spiritual needs.

Meanwhile, the New Zealand High Commission had changed beyond all recognition. During the war, it had expanded, and our original offices in the Strand could no longer contain the extra staff. Consequently, we had to rent more space in Halifax House, a spacious building just off the Strand, largely occupied by the U.K. Government. This was a time of expansion for New Zealand, and representatives from all its Government departments proliferated. As I have said, the New Zealanders were a pleasure to work with. If they had one failing, it was that they were somewhat parochial. They were firmly of the opinion that the world revolved around New Zealand, but they couldn't be faulted for that. I remember, on one occasion, overhearing a New Zealand visitor, a statuesque mature lady, talking to our cashier, who was a Londoner born and bred. After an exchange of pleasantries, the lady asked the inevitable question. "Tell me," she said. "Are you a New Zealander?" "Well, no, I'm afraid not," replied the cashier. There was a slight pause before the lady said, consolingly, "Oh! Oh well, never mind."

Although still a comparative junior, I was given the task of supervising the repatriation of countless New Zealand servicemen and their families, most of whom were English war brides. Almost all the berths on the many vessels plying between the United Kingdom and New Zealand were allocated by the New Zealand Government, and I had the unenviable job of deciding who should go first, working within various defined priorities. This had to be carried out with scrupulous fairness. Inevitably, there was some bad feeling, since everyone felt that they should have priority. My office was often filled with crying women and children pleading their case. In the interests of trade, a few businessmen were given priority. I remember one unpleasant individual who insisted on treating me to lunch at the Savoy, hoping to bribe me into giving him a berth. When he did not succeed, he complained bitterly to the High Commissioner, who managed to defend my decision and, at the same time, placate the would-be passenger.

I must have carried out my duties only too well because my job was up-graded and given to a fellow worker who claimed seniority. I was relegated to the finance branch where, after my initial disappointment, I settled down quite happily to pursue my career. Soon afterwards, the New Zealand Government decided to operate an ambitious scheme to attract migrants from the United Kingdom, and a large new department was created in London. Skilled tradesmen and others were offered passages for just sixty-four pounds per head. Conditions on board the ships were not too comfortable, and passengers had to endure sleeping in dormitories each containing sixteen or more berths, the men being separated from their wives and children.

At the end of the war, the power of the unions was growing, consequently the locally-recruited workers in the New Zealand High Commission formed their own staff association. The committee was at pains to assure the High Commisioner that this body was not a union but an association working to serve the interests of both the staff and the employers. The main tasks of the committee were to negotiate an annual pay rise and organise various social events. Before the war, we had enjoyed what was known as a Sports Day, when the office virtually closed down while the staff made their way to the Maori Club at Worcester Park. Wives and families were welcome and various activities were organised. These included a cricket match, a tug-of-war and races for the children and adults. This proved rather too tame for the returning servicemen, and the Sports Day was superseded, first by a boat trip on the Thames and later by an excursion to the seaside. The first of these excursions, which I helped to organise, was a great success, and these outings continued for some years. Initially, everyone travelled in coaches laid on by the committee, but, as people became more prosperous, some of the staff opted to travel in their own cars. In time, this served to undermine the whole purpose of the event and, eventually, it was quietly abandoned.

We had a dramatic society which produced one show a year, either a variety concert, at which our younger members could let their hair down, or, more often than not, one of the many farces popular in those postwar days. These shows took place at the old Cripplegate Theatre in the City and were well-attended. I was usually the box office manager, although I also took a minor part in some of the concerts. I remember one occasion which caused considerable embarrassment. One of our lady members, of uncertain years and somewhat less than attractive, appeared as a ballerina, dressed in traditional style. The audience was not sure whether her act was meant to be serious or a comic take-off, and there was an awkward silence, but by the time they had made up their minds she had made way for the next performer.

There were some real characters amongst our staff. One long-serving officer habitually returned from lunch in a drunken stupor. His colleagues always covered for him and he lived to enjoy a long retirement. Another staff member operated a successful antiques business in his spare time, and sometimes in his employers' time. One enterprising member actually organised the building of several houses and occasionally worked on the site himself, taking advantage of his sick leave entitlement. In my earlier days, the shipping officer was a pompous, well-meaning man, a strict Quaker and totally honest. However, his scruples did not prevent him from slipping out of the office for a quick haircut in the firm's time. Much of his work involved long telephone conversations with Liverpool and other ports. Being somewhat deaf, he used to bellow down the telephone. His colleagues maintained that he did not want a telephone, he need only have opened the window and shouted to be heard in Liverpool. One seconded officer tried to curry favour with his staff by presenting each of them with a woven mat imported from New Zealand. We were summoned to his office in strict order of seniority to choose our mat. I wouldn't like to say whether his generosity produced the required effect.

Peter and Jennifer in 1951

6

Sidelines

In the Summer of 1949, Dorothy and I decided to have a second baby. We carefully planned that he or she would be born just before the end of the income tax year so that I could claim an allowance for the whole year. However, there were complications, and the baby (Peter) arrived just two days too late. It took me a long time to forgive him but at least he avoided being born on April Fool's day. He was a perfect child for the first few months, but the Summer of 1950 was exceptionally hot and he became fractious for quite a time. However, our respective parents lived quite close and they were willing and able to help cope with the two children in their early years.

Although I was in secure employment and reasonably well paid, I decided to try to find some way of supplementing my income. Ever since I was a small boy I had been interested in films, and I felt that there was money to be made in presenting film shows for children at birthday and Christmas parties. The price of a 16mm sound film projector powerful enough for my purposes was around two hundred pounds, and I didn't have that sort of money to spare. However, I persuaded my father, my father-in-law and an uncle to loan me enough to get started. I found out all I could about film libraries and had some handbills printed. It was hard work at first and there was very little profit to be made because I didn't own a car and had to use taxis to transport my heavy equipment. Later I was fortunate to find a neighbour who was prepared to supply transport at a reasonable price. Gradually, I built up a clientele and began to break even. After re-paying my loans I managed to buy a secondhand car which, of course, made life a lot easier. Most of my engagements were around Christmas time when I was often called upon to present two programmes on Saturdays, sometimes at locations some considerable distance apart, which called for detailed advance planning. I must say that I enjoyed giving shows for children. The programmes usually lasted about an hour and consisted of five or six slapstick comedies, cartoons and animal films. When I could afford it, I always used to include a Mickey Mouse or Tom and Jerry colour cartoon to end the programme, and these were enthusiastically received.

However, there were times when I did not feel too well-disposed towards my young audiences. On one occasion I was using a brand new and expensive glassbeaded screen, when towards the end of the show I was horrified to see a dark stain appear near the bottom of the screen. When I had a chance to examine the damage it seemed that a child in the front row had spat on the screen. I was never able to repair the damage to my satisfaction. Another time, an almost new loudspeaker crashed to the ground after a child caught his foot in one of the cables, although I had done my best to keep them out of reach. Fortunately, I was able to repair the damage, although that piece of equipment was never quite the same again. One of the benefits of my new hobby was that our children always enjoyed film shows at their birthday parties. I was so full of enthusiasm in the early days that I removed two bricks from the wall separating our lounge from the dining room, despite my wife's protestations. This enabled me to operate the projector from the dining room and beam the picture onto a screen in the lounge with great success.

Most of my shows took place in the winter months when the weather created some hazards. I remember once being booked to give a show for the children of the local police. On the appointed day the weather was atrocious and there were heavy falls of snow. I could not get my car out of the garage and telephoned the police to give them the sad news. Not wanting to disappoint the youngsters, they laid on a special police car to take me and my equipment to the hall, where the show was a great success. As I became more well-known I was asked to show films to many organisations, including golf clubs, motoring clubs and even religious bodies. These provided their own special films, while I supplied and operated the projection equipment. I was employed by travel agents and tour operators to show films of their holiday programmes at many locations in the London area. Collecting and delivering the films sometimes led to problems. I had to arrange this work so that it did not interfere with my full-time job at the New Zealand High Commission, and on many occasions my lunch hours were devoted to visiting film libraries. If I had an engagement to fulfil in the early evening on work days, I used to drive my car, loaded with films and projection equipment, to a parking space convenient to New Zealand House. Fortunately, the car was never broken into, and this was in the days before parking meters. Such an arrangement would be impossible under present circumstances. At one time I was engaged by the local education authority to show travel films at evening classes. It was not a well-paid job but I enjoyed it, and those, mainly pensioners, who had enlisted for the series of lectures were very appreciative. I even negotiated a contract with Lambeth Borough Council to show films at the town hall on Monday afternoons and evenings throughout the winter. The films were provided by the Council, and my job was to use both my projector and another belonging to them. Changing from one projector to the other without interrupting the film called for exact timing and I became an expert in this operation. Getting time off from the office to give these shows wasn't easy and I had to use some of my annual leave entitlement for this purpose. I continued to give film shows until 1963, when a slipped disc put paid to my activities in that field. Reluctantly, I disposed of my equipment, which had served me so well over the years. During that time I had acquired only a very basic knowledge of the projector, and on the rare occasions when it broke down I hadn't a clue as to how to repair it. Although there were some near disasters at times, I suppose that I was very lucky in the circumstances. Anyway, with the advent of television, the days of film shows were numbered.

In 1953 my dear mother died prematurely from cancer. It was a great blow to us all, particularly my father, who had postponed his retirement in order to enhance his pension. Tragically, my mother's death put paid to his plans. He shared a home with one of my aunts for a time but then went to live in a retirement home in Putney. Our semi-detached house was too small to accommodate him but we visited him every week-end and made sure that he was as comfortable as possible. To add to our problems, my father-in-law died a few months later and we had to cope with the trauma of caring for his widow.

Once the film shows were well-established, I had decided to start up a new venture. When the children were small, we had spent several happy holidays in Birchington-on-Sea, not far from Margate. This was a favourite seaside village for many families, and it seemed to me that there was a need for more self-catering accommodation in that area. With Dorothy's full co-operation, I bought a detached three-bedroom bungalow within easy walking distance of the village and Minnis Bay. The intention was to let this property for the Summer months and to enjoy using it ourselves as and when the opportunity arose. My wife and I spent our week-ends putting the bungalow into good order and furnishing it with the essentials. After I had advertised in "The Lady" and published the details in the New Zealand House staff magazine, bookings started to pour in. I issued a brochure in which I described the bungalow as available to "selected" clients. They were, of course, selected according to their ability to pay the rent. Many of my clients were office colleagues who could be trusted to treat the property responsibly, and they returned year after year. At first, our children were thrilled to be able to visit the seaside so frequently, but as they grew older the novelty wore off. Nevertheless, we had some very enjoyable times together and were often joined by various friends and their offspring.

Meanwhile, considerable developments were taking place at the High Commission. As I have said, the old building in the Strand had become far too small for our needs, and in 1949 plans for a new building had begun to take form. The first step was the acquisition of the lease of the Carlton Hotel site and the adjoining His Majesty's Theatre (now Her Majesty's), but it was not until 1959 that the tender for the new building was placed. Much delay was caused by the fact that the proposed structure would be seventeen storeys high and would overlook Buckingham Palace. The authorities were worried that the Queen might be upset at this intrusion of her privacy. However, this objection was finally overcome. Since then, attitudes have changed considerably and there are now several very tall buildings within a stone's throw of the Palace with close-up views of its gardens. The move from the Strand began early in 1963 and the Queen was scheduled to open the new building on 9th May that year. By now I had been promoted to Purchasing Officer and life had been proceeding normally, until early in 1963 when I began to suffer from a slipped disc. This meant that I was absent from work for a full eight weeks. At one time I thought that I would never walk again but, thankfully, I made a complete recovery. My father had been ill for some time, and it was left to Dorothy to make the long and tedious journey by bus from Streatham to Putney since I was out of action and she did not drive. I was about to act as a steward for the opening of New Zealand House when I received a telephone call to say that my father was dying, and so I had to miss the ceremony. He passed away that evening, exactly ten years to the very hour after my mother had died.

New Zealand House, Haymarket, was a truly magnificent building. It had been designed to provide an administrative and social headquarters for the High Commissioner and his staff, and instead of the cramped conditions in the old building we now had ample space. There was a restaurant, used jointly by the staff and by visitors from New Zealand, where the standard of food was excellent. There were spacious reception areas on the lower floors and a magnificent ballroom where many functions were held, including the staff Christmas parties. At one such event, the audience was captivated by a beautiful young singer, then unknown. Her name? Kiri Te Kanawa. There were many facilities for the considerable number of New Zealanders who used the building for social purposes. It had cost around two million pounds to build, and the taxpayers made sure that they had their fair share of what was on offer. From the roof terrace there were marvellous views right across London, and visitors took full advantage of this opportunity to photograph the city.

This happy state of affairs continued for some years until the United Kingdom joined the Common Market. Before then, New Zealand had been able to sell its meat, wool, fruit and dairy products to this country. For one hundred years it had been cultivated as a larder for the mother country, but now all that was to change. Strict quotas were established to limit the import of its products, and New Zealand felt, rightly in my opinion, that it had been betrayed. It had to look for other markets for its products and this led to a weakening of its ties with the United Kingdom. The substantial orders for steel and other products which had always been placed in Britain now went mainly to Japan and, to a lesser extent, to Europe. While the mission in London was the first and largest of New Zealand's posts abroad, this was now affected by the growing prominence

51

of the E.E.C. in Brussels. Over the ensuing years New Zealand's economy suffered and there was less money to spend on overseas representation. The number of seconded officers was gradually reduced and many locally-recruited staff were made redundant. The happy atmosphere we had enjoyed for so many years virtually disappeared. The pensioners, most of whom had served loyally for a forty-year term, lost the privilege of holding their annual re-union lunch at New Zealand House, while the staff association virtually ceased to exist. At the present time the High Commission staff has been reduced to around thirty and occupies just a tiny proportion of the building. Plans have been made to turn the former staff restaurant and the ballroom into offices for letting to commercial enterprises, but at the time of writing the future of the whole building is uncertain. There is even the possibility that it may be sold.

I served under a number of High Commissioners, some good, some not so good. None could measure up to Bill Jordan, of course. A few were extroverts and served New Zealand well, while others were eccentric, to say the least. I remember one who insisted on going out to a local teashop every day to buy a sticky bun to eat with his mid-morning coffee, while his wife spent much of her time knitting in his office. However, the office of High Commissioner was a political appointment and invariably led to a knighthood. The succession of Chief Purchasing Officers also numbered some characters among their ranks. One such was a deeply religious man who spent a lot of his time working as a lay preacher. In his position, he was constantly being showered with gifts from our various suppliers, and he was not above indicating to them exactly what he would expect to receive.

New Zealand House, London

53

7

Home and Abroad

While all this was going on, life in Streatham was following a fairly predictable pattern. We sent Jennifer to nursery school hoping that we would be able to have her privately educated, but in the event we could not afford the fees, so she attended the local state primary school, which had a pretty good reputation, anyway. Three years later she was joined by Peter, and they both settled down quite happily to the routine of school life. The headmaster was popular and efficient, although I did not agree with some of his ideas. For example, he placed little importance on spelling, whereas I felt that to be able to spell properly was essential. However, we got on quite well together and I served for some time as deputy chairman of the parent-teacher association. In due course, both children won places to grammar schools, Jennifer at St. Martins-in-the-Fields High School, and Peter at my old school, Westminster City. By the time they reached their teens they were both very active in school life. Despite her small stature, Jennifer became tennis captain, while Peter was involved with the naval cadet force and the hockey team. At the age of eighteen Jennifer entered teacher training college, where she was to spend the next three years.

In the same year Dorothy and I celebrated our Silver Wedding. We felt that we ought to mark this special occasion in some way, and so we decided to book a cruise to the Canaries. Dorothy had never ventured abroad before, although I had travelled extensively (but far from comfortably) during my war service. Shortly before we were due to sail, just after Christmas, I had a recurrence of back trouble, and it was doubtful if I would be fit enough to travel. However, with the active support of our children and Jennifer's boyfriend, we managed to make it to Waterloo Station where we joined the boat train. It was bitterly cold and we were glad to reach Southampton and embark in our ship, the Stirling Castle. Once on board, we were told that our accommodation

R.M.M.V. "STIRLING CASTLE" (25,554 TONS)

UNION CASTLE
LINE

R.M.M.V. Stirling Castle

had been up-graded, and we were allocated a cabin one deck higher than we had expected. We found later that this was to be the vessel's last voyage before being broken up and our original cabin had already been stripped out. We were flattered to receive an invitation to the Captain's cocktail party. In our ignorance we didn't realise that everyone was invited. I had always suffered from travel sickness, and the first two days out from Southampton, as we crossed the Bay of Biscay, were most uncomfortable, to say the least. On the third day I emerged from our cabin and began to take a better view of life. The weather was warm and sunny for the rest of the voyage and we found the ports of call very interesting. During our brief sojourn in Tangier on the north African coast, Dorothy was even persuaded to take a camel ride. We thoroughly enjoyed our first joint experience of overseas travel and this was to be the first of many foreign holidays.

However, for the next few years we confined ourselves to brief breaks in Scotland, Wales and other parts of the U.K. Jennifer had, by now, completed her teacher training and joined the staff at a primary school not too far away. She married her long-time boyfriend in 1969 and they were fortunate enough to find a house in Streatham Vale. Meanwhile, Peter had completed his education, doing well in both his GCSE and A-level exams. He was offered a job with British Telecom and thus began a career which would lead him to senior management. By now, Dorothy and I had lived in Streatham for twenty-three years. We began to have itchy feet and considered the possibility of moving to Birchington, where we already had a holiday bungalow. Such a move would mean my commuting to London for the next eight years until my retirement; it was a journey of seventy-five miles each way. Jennifer was off our hands, but Peter was still living with us and working in the City. He had become engaged to his one-and-only girlfriend, Anne, and they planned to get married in 1971. We came to an arrangement whereby Peter moved in with his sister and her husband for a year or so until he married and found a house to share with Anne. We gave Jennifer a weekly sum for accommodating him (she was glad of the money) and it all worked quite well. This cleared the way for us to move to Birchington, which we did in 1970.

We had sold our original bungalow and now took up residence in a more spacious property conveniently situated just fifty yards from the sea at Minnis Bay. So began a somewhat punishing routine which was to last for several years. Every week-day morning we rose before six o'clock and I was on the train for London at seven. Although I left the office early (at four-thirty), I did not reach home until six-thirty at the earliest. In those days, however, the train service was pretty reliable, although inevitably there were occasions when delays occurred. On one memorable winter day I arrived home at ten p.m., having travelled endlessly through the Kent countryside. However, we regular travellers took it all in our stride and, incidentally, formed some lasting friendships. When I began commuting the annual season ticket cost me just over two hundred pounds; now it it costs over two thousand.

Dorothy had to resign herself to a very long day. The housework was usually finished by nine a.m., but she found plenty of things to occupy her time. To start with, she had to see to the needs of her elderly widowed mother, who was installed in a nearby residential home. In addition, one of my aged widowed aunts had moved into the area. She lived alone in a flat, and although at first she was capable of looking after herself she was often in need of help with the shopping and cleaning. We tried to take part in the village life as far as possible, but for several months of the year I only saw Birchington in daylight at the week-ends.

In 1972 Jennifer's first baby, Mark, arrived and we had to shift to London for a week or so to help cope with the new arrival. Peter and Anne had married as planned and set up home in Streatham Vale, where their first offspring, Matthew, was born two years later. After a three-year gap, Mark was joined by a brother, Simon, while Matthew welcomed a brother, James, not long afterwards. Anne's last baby, David, put in a somewhat tardy appearance four years later. Living by the seaside, we were very popular with our children and grandchildren, who in their earlier years descended on us regularly for their Summer holidays. While we enjoyed having them, it was always something of a relief when they returned home. At the time of writing, the eldest grandson is twenty-two and the youngest fourteen, but they still visit us regularly, the older ones travelling from London in their own cars and usually accompanied by their current girlfriend. Mark has recently announced his engagement, and although he says it will be a long one, I suppose we can expect to become great-grandparents in the course of time.

In 1973 I was given the opportunity to visit New Zealand as the guest of the Railways Department, to which I was responsible for buying large quantities of permanent way material and rolling stock. I travelled first class on the Air New Zealand inaugural flight from London to Los Angeles, a most enjoyable experience. After spending two days in L.A., during which I visited Disneyland (a delight for young and old), I flew on to Auckland. I stayed there briefly with relatives, who had emigrated from England some time previously, before travelling to the capital, Wellington, to begin my tour of the Railways Department. It was the first time I had been apart from Dorothy since the war years and I was desperately homesick, although my New Zealand colleagues made me very welcome, even allowing me a free telephone call home. My visit was very worthwhile and lasted about two weeks. I returned to London just in time to experience a nationwide rail strike, which meant that I had to travel to Birchington by coach, leading to further delays. Now I knew I was back home.

Later that year, Dorothy decided to try another cruise, this time on the Oriana, a far more up-market ship than the Stirling Castle, and much larger. We cruised to the Mediterranean, calling at many wellknown places, including Athens, Izmir, Majorca, Alicante and Gibraltar, all of which proved most interesting. Life on board ship did not really appeal to us. Although there was no shortage of entertainment, and our fellow-passengers were pleasant enough, too much time was taken up with eating and drinking, with the consequence that by the time we returned home we had put on a lot of weight, albeit due to our lack of will-power.

Reading about, or looking at photographs of, someone else's holidays can become dead boring, so I will not burden you with full details of our travels abroad. However, perhaps you will allow me to write about some of the highlights of our very varied holidays. Our first destination, in the year following our Mediterranean cruise, was Norway. The journey to Bergen by air took just two hours. After touching down, we passed a building engulfed in flames, which illustrated the vulnerability to fire of the country's wooden structures. We found Norway truly beautiful, but although most of the natives spoke some English we did not feel particularly welcome. This was, perhaps, explained by the behaviour of some tourists. At one hotel I watched a large party of Japanese stuffing oranges into their pockets, much to the annoyance of the staff, after enjoying a substantial buffet breakfast. At one stage we travelled by ship from Stavanger to Bergen. According to our brochure, we were to have dinner with the captain, but in fact we were treated to an indifferent meal shared with a party of arrogant Germans. Also on board were many young students, most of whom were openly taking drugs, and we were only too glad to disembark.

In 1975 we ventured further afield, visiting the Eastern U.S.A. and Canada on a package tour. After the obligatory sightseeing in New York, including the Empire State Building and Radio City Music Hall, where we saw "The Sound of Music" for the fifth time, we travelled to Boston, thence to Canada and the Niagara Falls, returning to New York via Washington and Philadelphia. Our fellow travellers were indeed a mixed bag. We were intrigued by the behaviour of one of them, a solicitor, who paid frequent visits to the toilet at the rear of the coach. At first we assumed that he had a weak bladder, but it later transpired that he was an alcoholic and sought solace in the bottle. By the time we reached the airport to fly home he was in a sorry state, despite the efforts of his long-suffering wife to protect him. We made friends with a pleasant couple from Guernsey, and we still exchange Christmas cards with them almost forty years later, although we have met them only once during that time. Our visit to the location of the battle of Gettysburg was made in pouring rain, but our knowledgeable local guide insisted on describing the conflict in great detail, taking pains to point out every gun emplacement. By the end of the day we were heartily sick of this extended history lesson, and we longed to get back to the hotel. The Americans can't resist mixing history with commercialism. At the former residence of President Jefferson we were ushered into the dining room, the dominant feature of which was a magnificent table. The door closed and a taped commentary began. "Note the marvellous sheen on the table surface. You too can produce a similar

60

effect on your own furniture by using Gloco polish regularly. This amazing product is freely obtainable from most hardware stores." Sadly, the tour was marred by the rudeness of the American coach driver, who refused to co-operate with the courier and made life difficult. Needless to say, he received no gratuities when we parted company.

When I had visited New Zealand two years earlier I had been very impressed by its beauty and the friendliness of the people, to such an extent that I thought Dorothy should see it. So, in 1976, we flew some thirteen thousand miles to begin an extensive six-week tour of that pleasant land. We called in at Disneyland en route and marvelled at the film studios in Hollywood before arriving in Auckland. It is impracticable for me to describe our holiday in detail, but suffice it to say that it was all most enjoyable. The only real culture that New Zealand enjoys is that of the Maoris, and this is exploited to the full for the benefit of the tourists. Until quite recently, New Zealanders enjoyed a complete break from work at week-ends, when everything shut down except for leisure amenities. This led more than one comedian to declare, "I went to visit New Zealand last week-end but it was closed." One of the highlights of our visit was our (brief) ascent of the Fox Glacier. We were each equipped with fifteen-pound boots, a heavy mackintosh and an alpenstock and were guided to the lower slopes, negotiating various small streams enroute. We had been advised to wear warm clothing, but with our exertions we soon became overheated and were glad to shed our garments when we returned to civilisation. One day, we drove along a vast beach bordering the Tasman sea. Although it was named the ninety-mile beach it was, in fact, only sixty miles long. In all, we visited almost every part of the country, from Cape Reinga in the north to the harbour of Bluff in the extreme south. I must say that we lived well in New Zealand and this was only too obvious from the cine films I had taken which clearly showed our girth expanding as the tour progressed. We flew back home via Singapore, notable for its cleanliness and safety. Wrong-doers were punished so severely that very few offended a second time. There was plenty of employment for everyone but they were not forced to work. However, if they didn't work they didn't eat, it was as simple as that.

Our appetite for foreign travel had been thoroughly whetted by now,

George, Dorothy, The Taj Mahal and friends

and we decided to take a holiday in a somewhat more exotic country. We booked a package tour of India and Nepal, but this turned out to be more of an experience than a holiday, and things went wrong right from the very start. We travelled from Birchington by train only to find that the London taxis were on strike and that it was pouring with rain. We were faced with the problem of getting to Waterloo but, by a stroke of luck, we found a taxi driver who did not know that he should have been on strike and took us to our destination before withdrawing his cab from the road.

On arrival at Delhi airport I took a few shots with my cine camera, blissfully unaware that photography was forbidden. When unpacking at our hotel, I discovered that I had not switched off the camera; consequently, the motor had continued running, ruining the film. Glancing at my wristwatch, I found that the winder had fallen off. It was impossible to get any repairs done and I had to rely on my wife's watch for the rest of the trip. For the first two days we were laid low with "Delhi belly", which affected all our party. We soon found that the Indian hotel staff expected to be tipped for every service, however small. On our first night, we were awakened at midnight by a loud knocking on the bedroom door. On opening it, I was confronted by one of the staff asking if we would like any additional coat-hangers. We told him what he could do with his hangers in no uncertain terms.

Things began to improve when we left Delhi for the so-called "pink city" of Jaipur, where we visited the Amber Fort, grandly mounted on elephants. From there we travelled to Agra to see the Taj Mahal in both daylight and moonlight, an unforgettable spectacle. We eventually arrived at Varanasi, where we were confined to the hotel for our own safety as a riot was taking place in the town. Things had quietened down by the next day when we rose at five a.m. to take a boat ride on the sacred river Ganges. Even at that early hour, hundreds of people were bathing in the river, mingling with women doing their washing. We were told that the Ganges was free from germs, since they could not survive in the contaminated water. Some distance away were the ghats, where families took their dead to be burned on funeral pyres before casting their ashes into the Ganges.

Next we flew to Kathmandu, capital of impoverished Nepal, a fascinating place by any standards. Surprisingly, we were assured that we could venture anywhere after dark in perfect safety. We could not resist taking a flight to view Mount Everest, the country's most famous landmark. The weather was good, and I was allowed into the cockpit to film this most glorious sight. The highlight of our tour was a visit to the famous Tiger Tops Jungle Lodge. We were flown in a small aircraft to a grass landing strip in the jungle where we were met by a team of elephants for the two-hour ride to the Lodge. En route we encountered a large rhinoceros which the elephants encircled to enable us to capture it on film. The elephants fed on the tall grass as we progressed, being careful to dislodge the dirt from the roots by knocking the grass against their knees before eating it. We heard many tales about the intelligence of these great beasts. We were told that on one occasion a tourist dropped the lens from his camera into deep, muddy water, to his great dismay. The mahout, or driver, issued a command to his elephant, which promptly located the lens and returned it to its delighted owner.

The Tiger Tops Lodge had room for only forty guests and was an oasis of comfort. Built to conform with the landscape, and making use of natural local materials, our bedrooms nestled in the treetops and were lit by kerosene lamps, yet astonishingly had showers and flush toilets. We had hoped to see a tiger while we were at the Lodge, since buffalo calves were staked out regularly as bait at spots overlooked by blinds (or hides), but we were unlucky. Anyway, I'm not sure that I would like to have seen a tiger attacking its defenceless prey. In compensation, we did glimpse one or two enormous crocodiles.

We arrived back at Kathmandu too late to catch our scheduled flight to Delhi. This resulted in us missing our scheduled homeward flight, and we had to spend twelve hours in the restaurant at Delhi airport, refreshed only by tea and sandwiches for which we had to compete with countless flies. The young lady of indeterminate nationality who acted as our courier throughout the trip was less than competent, and we came to the conclusion that she was, in fact, a drug addict. Our troubles did not end when we eventually touched down at Heathrow, much later than scheduled. We just caught the last train to Birchington which should have reached there before midnight. However, track maintenance was in progress and we had to complete our journey by bus.

Finding a taxi in the early hours of the morning was impossible and we had to walk almost a mile, carrying two heavy suitcases, before reaching home and tumbling into bed completely exhausted.

8

Far Away Places

In 1978 I retired from the High Commission (more about that later), and that Summer we enjoyed a quiet holiday in the Scillies. It was, perhaps, too quiet, and apart from the daily boat trips from St. Mary's to the neighbouring islands, the only event of any interest was the illustrated lecture on birdlife given by the local vicar to boost church funds. We stayed at the best hotel on St. Mary's and rubbed shoulders with the rich and famous. Among the guests was a Scotsman who owned a whisky distillery and had holidayed in the Scillies every year for the past twenty years. Another guest was a jeweller who had flown in from Jersey with his wife in a private aircraft. To tell the truth, we were somewhat out of our depth, but they were all very friendly.

We were soon anxious to venture further afield and decided to take another cruise, this time of a rather different character. A ship called the "Uganda" was making an educational cruise around the Mediterranean in February 1979. On board were several hundred school children and their teachers, housed in dormitories, and about a hundred cabin passengers. We flew to Naples, where we toured Pompei before joining the ship. All went well as we set sail, but shortly after we had passed Capri a force ten gale blew up and things began to get very uncomfortable. The teachers had their work cut out to pacify their charges. Both my wife and I suffered severely from sea sickness and were confined to our cabin for a full two days. There were times when we thought that our last hour had come, but eventually the storm subsided. Unfortunately, the ship's progress had been delayed to such an extent that we were unable to visit Alexandria, and sailed direct to Haifa, where we visited Jerusalem and Bethlehem, now sadly commercialised. After calling at Limassol (Cyprus) and Nauplia (Greece), we sailed to Kotor (Yugoslavia), which was most impressive. Imagine our dismay when we read, just six weeks later, that an earthquake had destroyed the town almost completely. Our final port of call was Venice, which lived up to all our expectations.

Later that year we spent a week on the Isle of Man, but that turned out to be a disappointing holiday, chiefly because our hotel accommodation left a lot to be desired.

We had heard a lot about the attractions of the U.S.A., so we arranged to tour the Western States. We flew to Los Angeles, where I was promptly taken ill (tension probably, according to the doctor) and spent the first day of our holiday in bed. Fortunately, I made a quick recovery and was able to enjoy the rest of the tour. Our route passed through Palm Springs and Phoenix, and thence to the Grand Canyon, one of the seven natural wonders of the world. We flew over the canyon in a six-seater plane, piloted with complete confidence by a young lady. We had no fears at that time, but since then more than one such flight in that region has come to grief with some loss of life. Our next stop was Las Vegas, Nevada's largest city, dedicated to all forms of gambling. We had heard of the spectacular shows laid on by the hotels, and booked to see one of these. It was somewhat disappointing, as we were tightly packed, shoulder to shoulder, seated at tables at right angles to the stage. The meal was indifferent and we were distracted by a long line of topless chorus girls, whose gyrations did nothing to sharpen our appetites. Next we stayed in Yosemite National Park, truly a scenic wonderland. Unfortunately, Dorothy had a fall which damaged her left hand, and I had to cut up her food and feed her for some days. There was a private hospital in the Park where Dorothy received prompt and efficient attention from the doctors, who were concerned that we might sue them for damages, a common practice in the U.S.A. Our final destination was San Francisco, with its fogs, cable cars, Fisherman's Wharf, Chinatown, Golden Gate Bridge, many fine restaurants and beautiful parks. There was also the notorious Alcatraz prison, now just a tourist attraction.

The following year we stayed nearer home, taking a short holiday in the Channel Islands, which could be reached in less than an hour by air from Manston Airport, just five minutes from Birchington.

One of my aunts had emigrated to South Africa many years ago, and we thought it would be a good idea to visit her two surviving daughters, who were both living there with their families. At the time of our tour (1981) things were relatively quiet and there was no sign of the violence yet to come. After spending a few days with one of my cousins in Johannesburg, we entered the Kruger National Park, where we stayed in a rest camp for two nights, observing the great variety of wild animals living there. All safaris through the park had to be escorted and tourists were not allowed to leave the coaches. In a moment of madness, I volunteered to be filmed stroking a half-tame cheetah, held on its leash by its handler. Our courier told me later that in no way would he have acted so imprudently, since cheetahs were the most unpredictable of animals. After paying a brief visit to Swaziland, which contained nothing of any interest, we went on to Durban, a truly beautiful city. The hotels there were staffed by Indians, members of a large colony which had settled there. Apartheid was still enforced at that time, and the best beaches were signposted "Whites Only". We travelled by the Garden Route along the coast, calling in at East London to meet my other cousin and her family. We stayed a few days in Capetown, where we ascended Table Mountain and toured the city before boarding the Blue Train to return to Johannesburg, a twenty-four journey during which we enjoyed five-star luxury. Not surprisingly, bookings for this train had to be made twelve months in advance. During our three-week stay in South Africa we saw just one policeman and a handful of soldiers, who were making a routine check of vehicles. We ventured into more than one town peopled by blacks, who were all friendly and talkative. Many of the whites we met were concerned about how they were regarded by the rest of the world and felt that apartheid must eventually be abolished.

By the end of 1983 we had again developed itchy feet and felt it was time to pay another visit to our relatives in New Zealand. This time we travelled via Hong Kong, taking a short day trip to Macau and spending a few days in China. We went by train from Hong Kong to Guangzhou, some ninety miles away. There we stayed in a 2000-bed hotel in conditions that were less than comfortable. On each floor there was a formidable janitor to whom we had to surrender our room key whenever we left the hotel. The beds were hard and the sparse furniture had seen better days. There was a television but, of course, the programmes were all in Chinese, except on one occasion when we were delighted to watch a New Year's Day performance of orchestral music from Vienna. Our guide took us to the local zoo to see a moth-eaten panda, then we visited a commune, where we lunched with the head man on rather rubbery duck and various vegetables. We were shown round a typical shack built of mud bricks, with a well in the garden. Surprisingly, the dwelling was equipped with electricity.

We were glad to board the train to return to Hong Kong. There were very few Europeans aboard, almost all the passengers being Chinese on their way to the big city to buy all kinds of luxury goods unobtainable in their country. The carriages were equipped with television and spotlessly clean. Food and drink was served from a trolley at regular intervals. There was one alarming incident. A number of Red Guards were travelling to the border, and one of them said that he wanted to ask me some questions, which he had written down in a notebook. With some trepidation, I asked him what he wanted to know. The first was "Underline the adverbs in the following sentences". It transpired that this young man was learning English and was delighted to have the opportunity to speak to an Englishman. We spent the rest of the journey talking about his family and his job, parting on the best of terms when he left the train at the border.

After China, our visit to New Zealand was something of an anti-climax. Arriving just before Christmas, we found that there were less signs of the season's festivities than we had seen in Hong Kong. We went to church on Christmas morning with everyone in their Summer attire and the sun shining brightly. The atmosphere just didn't seem right, but this was not surprising as Christmas in New Zealand coincided with the Summer holidays. Most New Zealanders seemed to want to get Christmas out of the way so that they could go off to the coast.

So far, we had not ventured into Europe, but we felt the time had now come to see what was offering. We had heard a lot about Switzerland and decided that it would be well worth a visit. Our guide was an elderly but vivacious lady who had been running these tours for many years and knew her way about. We had been led to believe that the Swiss were highly organised, and this turned out to be quite true. The trains ran on time and were spotlessly clean, while the hotels were welcoming and efficient with excellent meals. In the course of our tour, mainly by train, we visited Lucerne, Interlaken, Davos and Zermatt, viewing the awesome Matterhorn and the Eiger.

Although I had been to New Zealand three times, I had never visited Australia and now felt that the time had come to remedy this omission. So, in April 1989, we set off on our twelve thousand mile journey. Perth, on the West coast, was the home of a friend who had been to school with several of my aunts, and who was almost one hundred years old. She had married an Australian soldier during the First World War and had lived in Australia ever since, bringing up her three children. Despite her many years' residence there, she never regarded herself as Australian, and after the death of her husband she flew to London every Summer, renting a flat in the heart of the capital and acting as guide to visiting Australians. These pilgrimages continued until she was well into her eighties, and she finally died at the age of a hundred and one, not long after our visit. After a short stay in Perth we flew on to Adelaide, which must be Australia's most beautiful city, with the widest streets I have ever seen. Our next stop was Melbourne, a fascinating mixture of old and new, including a Victorian railway station and an ultra-modern complex housing sports of all kinds to international standards. Not far out of town was Phillip Island, where at Summerlands Beach, every evening of the year, enchanting Fairy Penguins emerge from the sea after their day's fishing to return to their burrows within metres of enthralled onlookers – a fascinating sight which we will not forget for a long time.

One highlight of our tour was a week spent in Sydney, with its Harbour Bridge and unique opera house. We arrived during a storm, and over the next few days endured more than our fair share of rain. Believe me, in Sydney it really does rain. On Anzac Day, a public holiday and, incidentally, Dorothy's birthday, we arranged to visit the Blue Mountains, a spectacle everyone told us we must not miss. As we boarded our coach it started to rain, and this persisted all day. The mountains were shrouded in thick mist and we could see nothing, a most disappointing experience. Just before we left Sydney the weather improved, and we spent at least one day in a delightful little town called Manly, a short boat ride away. We found the Australians very friendly and by no means as resentful of "Pommies" as we had been led to believe. In fact, the only show of

Murau, Austria

antagonism came from a restaurant waiter, who told us that he was Scottish and resented being mistaken for an Englishman. The Australians in general reserved their resentment for the Japanese, who were in evidence everywhere and who were buying up large parts of the country, including even wild life parks and many other tourist attractions.

Our final visit was to Cairns whence we took an excursion to view the fabulous Great Barrier Reef, a truly great experience. The city itself was stifling hot when we were there and seemed to be in danger of over-development, offering a great variety of hotels and restaurants to suit all tastes. Not far away was the Daintree River, where we were able to watch giant crocodiles basking in the warm sunshine. We also toured a rain forest, where our guide pointed out a deadly poisonous bush which instantly killed anyone who touched it. Not surprisingly, no one put this to the test. After being entertained by a group of Aboriginal dancers, we were invited to take tea with their head man. Souvenirs were on sale, and I was amused to see that despite their apparently primitive way of life the natives were adept at using a calculator to work out their prices. We returned to London via Darwin and Bangkok, a long and tedious journey. Our discomfort was heightened by the fact that the aircraft's toilets had not been serviced at Bangkok. By the time we approached Heathrow, just two toilets were in working order to serve some four hundred passengers. However, all in all, our Australian visit was one of our best long-distance holidays.

Although we had seen some of Eastern Canada when we went to the U.S.A., we had promised ourselves that we would see the Rockies when an opportunity presented itself. In 1991 we felt that the time had come, so we flew to Calgary to start a two-week tour of Western Canada. We were given a guided tour of the town en route to our hotel, but after our long flight we were too tired to appreciate it. We travelled by road to Banff in the heart of the Rockies, where we spent two nights, only to be rudely awakened in the early hours of the morning by the piercing sound of a train siren. Nobody had told us that this town was a busy railway terminus. We spent several days touring the region, in the course of which we set foot on a glacier and saw a variety of wild animals, including moose, elk and brown bears. At last we reached Vancouver, an elegant seaport boasting the beautiful Stanley Park and many fine buildings.

It was there that we enjoyed a splendid production of "Phantom of the Opera" at the Queen Elizabeth Theatre. Although it was a matinée, most of the audience were smartly dressed in keeping with their elegant surroundings. It was with some reluctance that we left the city to return home after a very pleasant and disaster-free vacation.

During the second World War I had spent some months in Austria, and I wanted to show my wife something of the area where I had been stationed. We booked for a coach tour which, at one point, was scheduled to pass within seventy miles of the little village of Murau, where I had lived. As it happened, we were free to do as we liked on that particular day, so we left our party and ventured on our own to find Murau. Our courier and the hotel receptionist were very helpful and showed us the rail route, which involved just one change of train. I had spent some time previously brushing up my knowledge of German and this proved very worthwhile. At least I knew enough of the language to ask basic questions and make myself understood. All went well, and we spent several happy hours exploring Murau and its surroundings, which seemed to have changed little since my previous sojourn. That day was, in fact, the highlight of our tour, although we did spend another very pleasant day with one of my daughter's former school friends, who had married an Austrian and lived in Reith bei Seefeld with her husband and three children. I have to say that we enjoyed those two days far more than our guided tours of Vienna and the other cities we visited. Since that vacation we have confined our travel to England, and I feel that our days of long-distance travel have passed. These days, holidays abroad seem to be fraught with so much uncertainty and danger, to say nothing of the hassle at airports (coupled with the sad fact of my advancing years), that I'm inclined to think there's no place like home.

9

Retirement

I had always had an interest in property, and soon after we moved from London to Birchington I had an opportunity to buy a large seafront property divided into three flats. The owner was anxious to get rid of it and the price was very reasonable, so I managed to secure a mortgage and clinched the deal. My intention was to use the rent from the flats to pay the mortgage. The purchase had left me short of cash but I found a builder to carry out the essential repairs and spent all my spare time painting, decorating and generally putting the property into good order. I had no difficulty in letting the flats and my tenants were quite co-operative. For a year or so everything went well but then I began to find it difficult to meet all the expenditure necessary to maintain the property. Thus, I decided to put it on the market, but before doing so I mentioned this to a wealthy friend of mine who, to my great surprise and delight, offered to buy it. It was a cash deal and the price was around three times what I had paid for it, although capital gains tax took some of the profit. Some years later, my friend disposed of the flats, and he too made a profit of around three hundred per cent, so all ended well.

At last my long years of commuting to London came to an end and I finally retired from the High Commission in 1978 after forty years' service. For the first twelve months of my retirement I contented myself with decorating and generally improving our bungalow until everything was to our liking. I then felt that I needed something more to occupy my time, since I was only fifty-eight and reasonably fit mentally and physically. My interest in property had not diminished and I decided to approach one or two local estate agents for a job. I was turned down by the first two firms I contacted, but one of them told me that another agency was looking for some help. It was a small concern, comprising two joint owners and a typist/receptionist. One owner, a qualified surveyor, was in his seventies and anxious to retire. His partner had bought him out

Birchington-on-Sea in the present day

76

and was looking for assistance. I was interviewed by this gentleman, who offered me a job on a "commission only" basis. This suited me because I had a reasonable pension from my previous employer, and I was not dependent on my earnings from the estate agency. From the start, my new boss and I got on like a house on fire. He was a genial ex-public school character, full of charm and first class at public relations. He had held a responsible position with a leading brewery before taking early retirement and settling in Westgate, just two miles from Birchington. He was a prolific family man with seven grown-up children, and he enjoyed life to the full. Neither he nor I had any qualifications to operate an estate agency but he had plenty of useful contacts with local solicitors and the like. My boss was not good at handling money and was only too pleased to hand over the accounting to me, giving me a virtually free hand to organise our finances while he concentrated on selling properties. Our overheads were comparatively small, and so long as we could sell an average of one property each month we could keep our heads above water. Within a year I was able to evaluate houses reasonably accurately and was soon showing prospective buyers over the properties on our books.

When dealing with clients I adopted the attitude that I was not there to push them into buying but just to show them what was available. In other words, this was the opposite method to the "hard sell" practised by most estate agents – and it worked. While our relationships with both buyers and sellers were mostly pleasant enough, I soon learned that disposing of and acquiring property tended to bring out the worst in people. On more than one occasion we had difficulty in getting our commission once we had made a sale. Contrary to the public image of estate agents, I found that almost without exception they were honest and straightforward, bearing in mind the keen competition they had to contend with. Sadly, my boss's wife died towards the end of 1983. His enthusiasm for the business rapidly deteriorated and he reluctantly sold out. I was asked by the new owner to stay on as manager, but I declined as I felt that I would not be able to establish the same happy relationship with him that I had enjoyed with his predecessor. Anyway, I was about to qualify for the State pension, so I did not need to continue working for gain.

After a brief rest, I looked around for something else to occupy my mind.

Several of my friends were voluntary workers with the Citizens' Advice Bureau, a nationwide organisation set up by the Government in 1939 to give people advice and help with their problems, anticipating the outbreak of war. After the obligatory period of training, I joined the Birchington bureau as a fully-fledged adviser. I wasn't very happy at first, since most of our clients in the village were old people with relatively minor problems, so I arranged to transfer to the Margate bureau, which was far busier. Thanet is a depressed area with high unemployment; consequently there was no shortage of people with problems. I spent six hours each week at the bureau dealing with an unending procession of clients. It was somewhat frightening at first, having to give advice on an enormous variety of enquiries, ranging from unemployment to social security problems. However, once I was able to find my way around the vast array of booklets and publications supplied by government agencies and the like, it became easier. My fellow workers and I had to ensure that our advice was impartial and confidential and available to all, irrespective of their circumstances. One thing I learned was that very many of the problems encountered were, in fact, self-inflicted, but I was not there to pass judgement. At times we had to face verbal and physical violence, but mostly we found that the clients appreciated our help and advice. I served with the bureau for almost ten years before deciding that I had had enough.

10

Man of Music

I'm one of the most unlikely persons ever to have become a composer. I don't come from a musical family, I don't play a musical instrument; in fact, I can't even read music. But apart from those minor drawbacks I'm well qualified to compose. For me, it all began in the spring of 1982 when the Falklands conflict was taking place. Like most people, of course, I used to spend my evenings watching the TV news bulletins, and as I saw what was happening out there I thought that something should be done to make a lasting record of our men's experiences. The idea of writing a song came to me. At first, I thought of writing something like "It's a Long Way to Tipperary" or "We'll Meet Again", but then I thought that perhaps something more serious was called for. So I thought up a tune, scribbled down some appropriate lyrics and sang the song, which I called "Song of The Task Force", on to a tape. I felt that the time had come for me to share my new-found talent with the rest of the world, so I sent the tape to the B.B.C. Nothing happened – there was no response whatever. I shouldn't have been surprised, because my unaccompanied rendering of the song was hardly inspiring. I was very despondent at this lack of interest, and my mood wasn't helped by an aunt of mine who had been sceptical from the beginning. She kept asking me what progress I was making, and I had to admit that I wasn't getting anywhere. At last she said, consolingly, "Oh, well, never mind. Sometimes even people with talent don't get anywhere".

I have two very good friends who live in Broadstairs. Their names are Bob and Rosemarie, and they are closely involved with the ActionAid charity which helps children in the Third World. When I played them the tape of my Falklands song, Rosemarie said "Why don't you write a theme song for the ActionAid charity?" "All right," I said. "I will." And I did, calling it, not surprisingly, the "ActionAid Song". Bob persuaded another of his friends, a talented musician, to write down the music of my songs in manuscript form, so now at last I had some sheet music.

I wasn't very interested in the ActionAid Song at that time, but I did want to promote my "Task Force" song, so I went round Thanet trying to find a singer or a choir to perform it, but met with no success. Then I had the brilliant idea of finding someone who would sing the song at a forthcoming talent contest at the Winter Gardens, Margate. I enlisted the help of a local newspaper, which put me in touch with an ex-professional singer with a very fine voice. He agreed to sing "Task Force" at the talent contest, but sadly he was un-placed. However, he did sing very well and I made a tape of his performance which was very impressive. I sent the tape to Radio Medway, as it was then known (it's now Radio Kent, of course), but again nothing happened. So I telephoned the Director of Programmes and asked whether he had received my tape.

"Yes, I've got your tape," he said, "but everyone' s writing songs about the Falklands."

I don't know about you, but I've never ever heard another song about the Falklands.

"Look, I'll tell you what I'll do," he said. "I'll put your tape on one side and, should a suitable opportunity occur, I'll broadcast it".

I knew what that meant. He'd put it on a shelf somewhere and it would lay there gathering dust and would never be heard again. Then I read in the national press that there was to be a victory parade for the Falklands conflict, so I rang up the Director of Programmes again and said, "There's to be a victory parade in October. Why can't you broadcast my song on the day of the parade?" I must have caught him off-guard because he couldn't think of any reason why he shouldn't broadcast it. So, on the day of the parade, my "Task Force" song was broadcast to an estimated audience of sixty thousand people. Instant fame, I thought. But nothing happened. Not one of those sixty thousand listeners bothered to make any comment.

By this time I was getting desperate to publicise my work, and I decided that the only thing to do was to produce a record of my two songs. Recording "Task Force" presented no problem. I had a singer and a pianist and found a recording studio in Herne Bay. Recording the "ActionAid Song" wasn't so easy. What I needed was a large choir of small children, and I didn't know that many children. My friend Bob came to the rescue. His son was, at that time, a pupil at the St. Lawrence College Junior School in Ramsgate. Bob spoke to the headmaster, who consulted the music master, and they decided that the whole school should record the song. They rehearsed for three weeks and then a date was fixed for the recording. Now, the headmaster was very publicity-conscious and he had not only arranged for the local press and radio to be present, but had also, by some miracle, persuaded TVS to film the recording. They sent a convoy from Maidstone with recording engineers, lighting experts, a couple of dolly birds to arrange interviews – the lot. There were 135 children in all, 130 small boys and 5 small girls (the school had just started taking girls), and they sang their hearts out for two hours while the song was recorded for TV. When it was over I was told that the recording would be shown on the "Coast to Coast" programme the following week. Now, I had never seen this programme before, but from then on I became an avid viewer. In due course the item was shown. Although the recording had taken two hours and had no doubt cost TVS a considerable sum of money, when it came on the screen it lasted for just under ninety seconds. Part of that time was taken up with interviews, so the "ActionAid Song" had hardly any coverage. Nevertheless, I was impressed with the recording; in fact I must have had a brainstorm, because I ordered two thousand copies of the record. Now, to someone like Bob Geldof two thousand records is a drop in the ocean, but to me it was an awful lot of records. Rosemarie volunteered to dispose of half the records through her ActionAid channels, leaving me to sell the rest. By the way, the idea was that if we made any profit from the record sales (which we didn't think was very likely), we would donate the money to the South Atlantic Fund and to ActionAid.

In an attempt to get maximum publicity for the "Task Force" song, I sent complimentary records to a number of people in high places. starting with Prince Andrew and working my way downwards through Mrs Thatcher, Sir Rex Hunt (the Falklands Civil Commissioner) and the heads of the armed services who had conducted the campaign. Of course I didn't raise any money for my efforts, but one result was that the record was played regularly on the Falklands Radio. For the next few months I

81

worked hard to sell the record, even at one stage acting as a door-to-door salesman in Birchington. I was able to more or less blackmail my friends and neighbours into buying a copy but it proved more difficult to persuade other people. However, Rosemarie and I eventually sold almost all the 2,000 records and made a profit of £400 which was divided equally between the two charities I have mentioned. So it was all worthwhile.

You may wonder how my family reacted to my new-found talent. My Wife was totally supportive, as always. I wouldn't get far without her help. My two children, a boy and a girl, both now in their early forties, thought I had gone mad. My five grandsons – with one exception – were completely indifferent. Now, I do not allow myself to favour any one particular grandson. I think this would be morally wrong. So I treat my grandsons all equally – no favourites. But I can't help thinking that the one who likes my music must be, without doubt, the most intelligent of the lot. Mind you, I'm not sure how far his appreciation of music has developed. When he was about six years old, I took him to see a pantomime – "Dick Whittington" – at the Winter Gardens, Margate. When it was over, I asked him which part of the show he had enjoyed the most. Without any hesitation he said, "The part I liked best was when the microphone kept popping up through the hole in the stage."

Once the Falklands conflict was over, I turned my attention to matters nearer home. We have a very strong Residents' Association in our village, and its chairman had complained in the quarterly magazine that members were not taking enough interest in local affairs – there was too much apathy. I thought that perhaps the best way to foster a community spirit would be to write a song which could be adopted as a sort of signature tune. And so I composed a number called "Birchington-on-Sea". This tells of the idyllic life we lead in our village where the school children are all polite and courteous and the shopkeepers are friendly and helpful – if you believe that, you'll believe anything. The song met with some success and has, in fact, been adopted by the Parish Council as the village's theme tune.

About that time Chas and Dave, the cockney duo, were becoming very popular in this area, having written a song called "Down to Margate". No doubt you have heard it. Some of you may even like it – there's no accounting for taste. I was somewhat jealous of their success, so I decided to write a song about Thanet, of which Margate is a part. The District Council was, at that time, encouraging us to talk about Thanet, not Broadstairs, Margate and Ramsgate. More recently, we've been told to forget Thanet and talk about Kent's Leisure Coast – whatever that is. And so I composed "Thanet Forever", which describes the many attractions of this area. In my innocence, or ignorance, I was foolish enough to think that Thanet District Council would welcome my song as an aid to promote tourism. I played a tape of the song to their Leisure Committee and offered them the song free of charge. This, of course, immediately made them suspicious and they weren't sure what to do. After much discussion (the Committee had no fewer than twenty-six members), they decided in their wisdom that, while they liked the idea of a promotional song, there might be someone somewhere who could write a better song than mine. So they organised a "Song for Thanet" contest. I entered my contribution and promptly forgot about it. There seemed no point in waiting for the result of the contest, so I decided to produce a new record, this time of "Thanet Forever" and "Birchington-on-Sea". I had learned to be more cautious, so I ordered just one thousand copies. But, of course, there was only me to sell them, so I wasn't really much better off. I spent the Summer calling on pubs, clubs, gift shops and hotels throughout Thanet trying to persuade them to buy my record, and I had some success. Then in the Autumn the result of the "Song for Thanet" contest was announced. I was told I'd been awarded third prize. Well, the Council couldn't have given me first prize without losing face.

I was a bit disappointed at first, but then I learned that my prize consisted of gift vouchers from Marks and Spencers worth £25 and groceries from a local supermarket worth a similar amount. I was much happier. And I was even more pleased when the first and second prizewinners were each awarded a week in a holiday camp.

I thought that my "Thanet Forever" song was worthy of a wider audience, and so I sent tapes of the song to BBC Television, ITV and various radio stations. Not much happened at first, but one day the telephone rang and a voice said, "I'm Christopher Palmer, the producer of the 'Wish You Were Here' holiday programme on Thames Television.

I like your tune, but we've got no intention of coming to Thanet. Could you change the title of your song to "Britain Forever", and change the lyrics to delete all reference to Thanet?" "Certainly," I replied. "No problem!" – anything to get on television. So I sent Chris Palmer the revised lyrics for his approval. "That's great," he said. "Bring your band up to London and we'll re-record your song as "Britain Forever." Well, of course, I hadn't got a band, but I knew a man who had, and in due course the recording took place at Thames Television's Teddington studios. On March 19th, 1984, my song was played on television in the "Wish You Were Here" programme. It was networked to all the ITV regions and repeated shortly afterwards on Channel 4. An estimated fourteen million people heard the song and my name appeared in the credits. Well, I was over the moon. Instant fame was just around the corner. I couldn't go wrong. Nothing happened for two weeks and then I had a letter from Thames Television enclosing some fan mail. It consisted of two requests – *two* requests, not two million requests – for tapes of the song. One came from a lady whose daughter was emigrating to Australia and who wanted to give her something to remind her of the Old Country. The other was from an old-age pensioner who said his hobby was playing "the bones" to patients in a local hospital; he was obviously never short of raw material for his act. "Please send me a tape of your song," he wrote. "I'm sure that when I play it at the hospital the patients will all hop out of bed and dance round the ward."

I sent him a tape, charging him just the cost price, and soon afterwards I got a most enthusiastic reply. "It worked," he wrote. "They did hop out of bed and dance round the ward. I'm very grateful to you for the tape. Here's an extra ten pence for your kindness."

I continued my efforts to sell the "Thanet Forever" record – but some of the methods I used weren't too successful. On one occasion, a very cold October day, I spent eight hours in the foyer of the local supermarket, by kind permission of the manager, playing the tape over and over again on my portable player. At the end of the day I had sold a grand total of four records – and three of those had been bought by a friend of mine who was shopping there and felt sorry for me.

But I have the satisfaction of knowing that my music has been heard in many parts of the world – Australia, New Zealand, Canada, the U.S.A., Malta, Finland and, of course, the Falklands. In fact, I have penetrated even more remote territory. Just before Christmas 1983, my Wife and I spent a few days in China. Not many people speak English in China, but we were fortunate to have a very pleasant young lady as our guide. At the end of the tour I wanted to reward her in the usual way, but she refused to take any money – something to do with being Chinese, I think. However, by dint of careful questioning I discovered that she possessed a record player. By chance, I happened to have with me several copies of my "Thanet Forever" record. And so it came about that when we boarded the train to return to Hong Kong, we left behind a somewhat bemused guide clutching an autographed copy of the record. What the Chinese made of "Birchington-on-Sea" I shall never know.

Sometimes I am asked what inspires me to write a particular song. Well, it could be a childhood memory. When I was a small boy I was very fond of circuses. I still am, as a matter of fact, although I know it's not fashionable these days. So what could be more natural than for me to write a circus song? I called it "Circus Boy" and it tells the story of a boy who wanted to join the circus as a trapeze artiste, but he met a girl with whom he fell in love. He changed his plans, married, and got a job in an office – and his feet never left the ground.

Despite the fact that I have five grandsons, I'm still quite fond of children, and I have written several songs specially for them. One of the most successful is called "A Children's Carol", which has been sung in many churches and Sunday schools throughout Kent and London. Every year, Kent County Council organises a carol service for children who have what are described as learning difficulties. They are, in fact, physically or mentally disabled. The organisers chose my carol for inclusion in this service when it was held in Rochester Cathedral because they felt it had an attractive tune and simple words which the children could sing and understand. There were some six hundred children in the congregation, together with their parents and teachers. My wife and I were invited to attend, and we found it a most moving experience.

On one occasion I was invited to the wedding of the daughter of my wife's cousin, and I thought that I would write a song for the bride's father to sing to his daughter on the great day. It was called "To My Daughter" and was an instant success, becoming very popular with parents of prospective brides. A record of this song sold two thousand copies, enabling me to make a substantial donation to charity. Major Ferguson gave his daughter a copy when she married Prince Andrew, although it doesn't seem to have done her much good. Someone asked me how the Major got to hear about the record. The answer is simple – I wrote and told him about it.

About this time, I read in the national Press about a lady who had spent twenty thousand pounds on her daughter's wedding. She was not satisfied with the video she had commissioned and decided to re-stage the nuptials a few months later. I felt sorry for her and sent her a copy of my "To My Daughter" record as some small compensation for her disappointment. Within a few days the bride's mother telephoned to say how much she had enjoyed my song and to ask if I could arrange for the singer to attend the re-enacted wedding and sing the song live at the reception. I pointed out that this would not be practicable in view of the time and distance involved, Birchington being some two hundred and fifty miles from Torquay, where the ceremony was to take place. However, I offered to supply her with the words and sheet music, suggesting that she arrange for a local singer to perform the song. She was delighted with this suggestion and insisted that my wife and I should attend the reception at her expense. So we set off to Torquay on a very cold November day. Arriving at the church, we joined the hundred or so other guests, and the wedding service was re-enacted, but without the actual words of the ceremony. The bride and bridegroom left for the reception in a horse-drawn carriage and we followed in our cars to the same five-star hotel where the original reception had been held. I introduced myself to the bride's mother and asked if I could meet the singer who was to perform my song. "My husband has made all the arrangements," she said. "You'll have to ask him." I sought out the husband and asked him the same question. "Well, as a matter of fact," he said, "I'm going to sing the song myself." Apparently he had been having singing lessons, unbeknown to his wife, and had rehearsed the number with the band. Once the meal was over and the speeches had been made, the time came for the song. As soon as the husband began to sing, a look of horror came over his wife's face – not surprisingly, because he had no voice at all. He started flat and never got into the right key, completely ruining my song. When he had finished there was a round of polite applause from the guests, who must have felt sorry for him. I told him I admired his courage in attempting the song, but he said he felt that if anyone was to sing it to his daughter it should be him, which I suppose was fair enough. At the disco which followed the reception the record of "To My Daughter" was played, together with another song called "To My Father", which I had written for the bride to sing to her father as a sort of "thank you". They danced together to the music and it all ended on a happy note. The repeat wedding cost the bride's mother a cool ten thousand pounds, but it didn't seem to worry her. I found out afterwards that she owned a residential home for old people.

More often than not, weddings are followed in the course of time by christenings, although in this modern age sometimes the babies precede the marriage. My next step, therefore, was to write an appropriate song called "The Christening". A tape of this work has been presented to the parents and godparents of numerous babies. I've never discovered whether our Torquay bride has been blessed with children.

Sometimes inspiration for a new song is lacking. On one such occasion a friend suggested I should choose a girl's name as the title of my next work. I know very little about girls, but I thought it wasn't a bad idea and composed a number called "Sara", the first name that came into my head. Now what could be more innocent than that? But when I played it over to my wife her reaction was unexpected. "So who is this Sara?" she demanded to know. In vain, I explained that this girl was a figment of my imagination. "Why can't you write a song about me?" asked my wife. As you know, her name is Dorothy, not the easiest name to fit into a song. However, I overcame this problem, and the result was a song which I called "To Dorothy with Love", which I wrote to celebrate our fortieth wedding anniversary. As one gets older, the time seems to pass more and more quickly, and before we realised it we were celebrating our fiftieth anniversary. I felt that I should mark this occasion with a new song, but I saved myself a lot of effort by using the tune and most of the lyrics of "To Dorothy with Love". This time, however, I did not personalise the song by using my wife's name, but adapted the lyrics to apply to anyone celebrating such an occasion. Not surprisingly, I called this latest effort "Golden Wedding". My wife was delighted with this, and so were the many couples to whom I have since presented cassettes of the song to mark their own anniversaries. You might like to know that I sang "To Dorothy with Love" on Channel 4 television on St. Valentine's Day, 1993.

When I retired, I joined the Probus Club in Birchington. The Probus movement is a worldwide organisation for retired professional and businessmen, as the name implies. My fellow members knew that I was a composer, and the Club secretary asked me if I would write a signature tune for the movement. I was flattered at this request and set to work to produce several alternative tunes from which he could take his pick. I arranged for the chosen song to be recorded by a local male voice choir and advertised it in the Probus magazine. There are some eight hundred Probus Clubs in the U. K. and many of them have bought cassettes with the intention of playing and/or singing "The Probus Song" at their monthly meetings. While the song enjoyed moderate success in this country it was received with much more enthusiasm in Australia and New Zealand, where there are some sixty thousand members. Before visiting Australia with my wife in 1989, I contacted several clubs there with the result that we enjoyed a lot of hospitality. I had devised a forty-minute humorous talk called "The Lighter Side of Songwriting", which was illustrated with short taped extracts from some of my songs. I gave this talk to several clubs and it was very well received. We were invited to attend a church service in Adelaide to celebrate the anniversary of the local Probus Club. The principal address was given by the Bishop of Adelaide, who had a delightful sense of humour. He told us of two occasions on which he was the victim of mistaken identity. Not long after he had been ordained, he was shopping locally when he was seen by a small boy who must have attended his church service the previous day. "Look, Mum. There's God," shouted the lad excitedly. On the second occasion, when he had been appointed a bishop, he was standing at the church door in all his regalia and holding his crook when he became aware of a small girl looking at him with great interest. "I know who you are," she said. Flattered by the apparent knowledge of one so young, the bishop said, "Well, who am I, then?" "Why, you're Little Bo Peep," she replied, triumphantly.

When my son, Peter, was at school, he learned to play the clarinet and one of his uncles gave him the nickname of Piccolo Pete. This prompted me to compose a lightweight number which I called "Piccolo Pete and the Band". This described the fortunes of a group which didn't last very long due to a series of misfortunes, and caused a lot of amusement.

In 1988 TVS (now Meridian Television) organised a fund-raising effort which they called "Telethon". I was surprised to be asked by a local trio (a boy and two girls) to write the lyrics for a song which they were to perform in this show. I spent a lot of effort writing three verses of lyrics, but by the time the song was televised I found difficulty in recognising my words. However, as the lead singer was unintelligible anyway, it didn't really matter a great deal. At least I had played a (very) small part in helping to raise some millions of pounds for various charities.

On my long return journey from the Torquay wedding, I began to feel the strain of driving for so long, and I said to my wife, "I'm fed up with this. I just wanna go 'ome." Once safely back home, it struck me that the phrase "I Wanna Go 'Ome" would make a good title for a Cockney song and, as it happened, it didn't take me long to think up a suitable tune and lyrics. Although this song has been performed locally it hasn't had the success I think it deserves, but at the time of writing I'm still hoping to persuade various singers (e.g. Max Bygraves, Tommy Steele, Chas 'n Dave) to give it a try.

You will see that the lyrics of all the songs I have mentioned in this chapter are set out in the appendices to this book.

When I first started composing, my friends were very sceptical. They told me that I would get nowhere, even if I had any talent (which they doubted), because the world of music was so competitive. Nevertheless, I persevered and have, perhaps, achieved something. I've made three records which have been played worldwide. I've raised over one thousand pounds for charity. I think I've helped to promote tourism in this area, although the local council might not agree. And I've been elected to membership of the Performing Right Society, which collects royalties for us poor, struggling composers. Last year they collected around one hundred million pounds worldwide. My share was fifty pounds. My fellow member, Andrew Lloyd Webber, got one and a half million pounds. So it seems I have some way to go yet.

I'm never allowed to become big-headed over my small successes, because I'm continually being cut down to size. I'll give you an example. Not long ago, I gave a talk on songwriting to a group of senior citizens in Margate. When I had finished, I noticed a little old lady hovering around, obviously wanting to speak to me. "Can I help you, madam?" I asked. "Yes," she said. "You live in Birchington, don't you? Well, I've got a flat in Arlington House on Margate seafront. You have to pass it on the way to Birchington – you can give me a lift. I usually take a taxi but you'll be quicker and it won't cost me anything." "Certainly, madam," I replied, ever the perfect gentleman. I bundled her into the car and dropped her off at Arlington House. "Thank you very much," she said "I've had a wonderful afternoon. I've really enjoyed it." I felt very flattered. "Well, thank you, madam," I said. "I'm very pleased to hear it." "Of course," she went on, "I'm almost stone deaf. I couldn't hear a word you were saying, but some of the music sounded quite nice."

I've told my wife that when I die I want my epitaph to read simply: "He Tried". In fact, I've already written my obituary (well in advance, I hope) in the form of a song – and here it is:

He Tried

Now I'll tell you the story of a man who couldn't win,
He worked so hard, he persevered, he fought through thick and thin,
Despite his best endeavours he didn't reach the summit,
More than once he slipped right back just when he thought he'd done it.
But he tried.

When George was born – an only child – his parents had ambitions,
They saw their son a great success, ensconced in high positions,
And while at school he studied well to meet their expectations,
The trouble was he found it hard to pass examinations.
But he tried.

When war broke out in '39 he joined up with the rest,
He had no stomach for the fight although he did his best,
He learned to be a soldier and prepared himself for action,
Applied for a commission, failed selection by a fraction.
But he tried.

For forty years he slaved away against great competition,
With regular promotion he was fired with fresh ambition,
The top jobs were within his grasp, he'd realised his potential,
His face, however, didn't fit – of course that was essential.
But he tried.

In later years, George tried his hand at musical composing,
He thought he'd write a hit or two, he found the work engrossing,
He sent his songs to publishers, his lyrics were quite clever,
Rejection slips came thick and fast – his name was *not* Lloyd Webber.
But he tried.

At last his long and happy life came to a peaceful end,
And those he left behind him really felt they'd lost a friend,
To various relations he bequeathed his small estate,
He would have taken it with him but he left it far too late.
'Though he tried,
How he tried.

THE END

The Family: Mark, Simon, Richard, Jennifer, George, Peter, Dorothy, Anne, David, Matthew, James.

92

Appendix 1

Task Force

We went a long way to fight, to fight against the foe,
Our cause was surely right, as everyone must know,
We did our best to win, comrades-in-arms were we,
We strove with all our might to earn our victory.
Now we'll come back home, away from the cruel seas,
Back to all our friends, back to our families.

Although the fight was hard and the road was rough
We had the fighting spirit that helped to make us tough,
We meant to reach our goal whate'er the odds might be,
We went to beat the foe and set our people free.
Now we'll come back home, away from the cruel seas,
Back to all our friends, back to our families.

The ActionAid Song

Verse 1
As we watch our girls and boys playing happily
We should give a thought for those who live in misery,
Many find it difficult to earn their daily bread,
Many, when a new day dawns, renew a life they dread.

CHORUS
We must help them, we must help them, children overseas,
Ever-loving, ever-giving, we must hear their pleas,
ActionAid is always working to fulfil their needs,
Give them the support they ask for – not just words but deeds.

continued...

Verse 2
You and I can eat our fill and we've lots of choice,
Others aren't so fortunate and they have no voice,
They are free to starve to death, they are free to die,
But we can give them comfort and their wants supply.

Chorus
As above

Appendix 2

Birchington-on-Sea

Verse 1
Down in North East Kent, close beside the sea,
Lies a thriving village for everyone to see,
It has a Village Centre where old folk like to throng,
They love to have a gossip and sing an old-time song.

CHORUS
Birchington, Birchington, village by the sea,
Proud of its traditions, symbol of the free,
Always in the forefront, enterprisingly,
We salute your progress, Birchington-on-Sea.

Verse 2
The youngsters aren't forgotten, they're helped in many ways,
We listen to their music and applaud their plays,
The shopkeepers are friendly and do their best to please,
The atmosphere is happy and everyone's at ease.

CHORUS
As above

Verse 3
Residents united in their Association
Maintain their independence with staunch co-operation,
Each year there is a Carnival with fun for everyone,
A time for celebration when all the work is done.

CHORUS
As above

continued...

Verse 4
We do our best to foster the entente cordiale,
The French are our near neighbours, we're twinned with La Chapelle,
But when the Winter comes our visitors have gone,
We look forward to Christmas, and give our thanks in song.

CHORUS
As above

Appendix 3

Thanet Forever

Verse 1
When you need a break or a day out at the coast
Come to North East Kent and you'll see why we can boast,
Lots of lovely sands and towering cliffs besides,
You can get a suntan, but don't forget the tides.

CHORUS
Thanet, Thanet, right beside the sea,
Broadstairs, Margate, Ramsgate, not one resort but three,
Fun for all the family, always lots to do,
Thanet forever, whatever the weather
It's just the place for you.

Verse 2
By car and coach and train they come from everywhere
To stroll along the prom and breathe the bracing air,
Amusements there are plenty, the kids are wide awake,
For Mum and Dad it's restful, and they enjoy the break.

CHORUS
As above

Verse 3
For young and old we cater, we do our best to please,
Everybody's happy and everyone's at ease,
When the day is done and it's time to go back home
You'll want to come again, so be sure you're not alone.

CHORUS
As above

Circus Boy

Verse 1

When I was a little boy I had a lovely gran,
I used to tell her what I'd do when I became a man,
I didn't want to drive a train or sail upon the sea,
This is what I'd tell my Gran when I went to tea.
I want to join the circus and swing from the high trapeze,
I want to fly right up to the sky and glide through the air with ease,
I want to be a hero, with folk all cheering me,
That's what I'll do when I grow up, just you wait and see.

Verse 2

Then I met a little girl as pretty as could be,
I fell in love with her, and she said she'd marry me,
I went to see my Gran again and said I'd changed my plans,
The sawdust ring had lost its charm, and I'd put up the banns.
So I didn't join the circus or swing from the high trapeze,
I didn't fly right up to the sky or glide through the air with ease,
I got a job in an office and made the daily round,
I was a model husband – and my feet stayed on the ground.

Appendix 5

A Children's Carol

Jesus Christ was born on Christmas Day,
Jesus Christ was born on Christmas Day,
Here with us on earth he came to stay,
When Jesus Christ was born.

Shepherds in the fields had seen the sign,
Shepherds in the fields had seen the sign,
They wondered what had caused the star to shine
When Jesus Christ was born.

As the Holy night gave place to day,
As the Holy night gave place to day,
To Bethlehem the shepherds made their way
When Jesus was born.

They came upon the stable where He lay,
They came upon the stable where He lay,
They saw the Baby lying in the hay
When Jesus was born.

"Glory be to God" the shepherds sang,
"Glory be to God" the shepherds sang,
With happiness and joy their voices rang
When Jesus Christ was born.

To My Daughter

Verse 1
My own dearest daughter, this is your day,
I'm proud, as your father, to give you away,
Your family and friends will be there to see
You gracefully walk up the church aisle with me.

CHORUS
Happiness, happiness, that's my wish for you,
Tenderness, faithfulness, these you'll need too,
Love your man, trust your man, always be true,
Remember this wedding day song.

Verse 2
There may not be sunshine, but it seems like June,
The warmth of your smile will make Summer come soon,
I'm sure you'll win through, dear, whatever Life brings,
Think of your happiness as the choir sings.

CHORUS
As above

Verse 3
The time has come now, dear, for you to leave home,
You're starting a new life but you're not alone,
Your Mother and I will be thinking of you,
God bless you and keep you, whatever you do.

CHORUS
As above

To My Father

Verse 1
Thank you, dear Father, for my wedding song,
That was a lovely idea,
I will remember it all my life long,
Though not without shedding a tear,
Gone are the days when I sat on your knee,
Your arms enfolding me so tenderly,
You gently taught me to know right from wrong,
I will be truthful and I will be faithful,
Thank you for my wedding song.

Verse 2
I'm still your daughter though I'm leaving home,
Don't think that you're losing me,
I will come back to you, but not alone,
I'll have my new family.
Happiness, happiness you have wished me,
Tenderness, faithfulness, I'll need all three.
This is the day I have hoped for so long,
Everything's marvellous, everything's wonderful,
Thank you for my wedding song.

The Christening

Verse 1
Since you were born, my darling child,
The world has seemed a better place,
Such is the joy you bring to us
When we behold your smiling face.
And now you are to be baptised,
A tiny miracle of love,
Our fondest hopes are realised
As we give thanks to God.   *continued...*

Verse 2
We've gathered here to wish you well
And tell you that we'll do our best
To help you meet Life's many trials,
And comfort you when you're distressed.
May you grow up to live in peace,
May God protect you day and night,
May you be strong, and never cease
To fight for what you feel is right.

Appendix 8

Sara

Verse 1
Now it all seems a long time ago
When we first met – I was so slow,
I didn't realise what love could mean,
I didn't see how it could have been.

CHORUS
Sara, Sara, why must you leave me?
Sweetheart, sweetheart, why must you go?
We could live happily,
Why can't you stay with me?
Sara, Sara, I love you so.

Verse 2
You were so young, so full of life,
My only aim was to make you my wife,
Something went wrong, I don't know what,
Now I am losing all I have got.

CHORUS
As above

To Dorothy With Love

Verse 1
It's now fifty years since you were my bride,
I still recall that moment with pride,
We were both young, and I loved you so,
When we were married, a long time ago.
Dorothy, Dorothy, girl of my dreams,
Dorothy – gift of God – that's what it means,
Since we met, long ago, decades have passed,
But we love each other still, true to the last.

Verse 2
Soon came the War, with Britain at bay,
When I came back after long years away
The white cliffs were there, though the birds were not blue,
But you were still waiting, faithful and true.
Dorothy, Dorothy, girl of my dreams,
Dorothy gift of God – that's what it means,
We have had happy times, troubled ones too,
But my life's been full of joy since I met you.

Verse 3
And so you gave me a daughter and son,
Then they grew up, and soon they were gone,
Now there's just us, just you and me,
Still happy together, close by the sea.
Dorothy, Dorothy, girl of my dreams,
Dorothy – gift of God – that's what it means,
Days may come, days may go, time passes fast,
But our love grows stronger still, long may it last.

Golden Wedding

Verse 1
It's now fifty years since you were my bride,
I still recall that moment with pride,
We were both young, and I loved you so
When we were married, a long time ago.
Sweetheart mine, sweetheart mine, girl of my dreams,
Tenderness, faithfulness, that's what love means,
Since we met, long ago, decades have passed,
But we are together still, true to the last.

Verse 2
When we were wed our hopes were so high,
Our way ahead seemed all sun and blue sky,
We didn't think there'd be stormclouds as well,
Sadness and problems we could not foretell,
Sweetheart mine, sweetheart mine, girl of my dreams,
Tenderness, faithfulness, that's what love means,
We have had happy times, troubled ones too,
But my life's been full of joy since I met you.

Verse 3
Over the years our family has grown,
Now they've left home and we're on our own,
Fifty years on, there's just you and me,
Happily living in close harmony.
Sweetheart mine, sweetheart mine, girl of my dreams,
Tenderness, faithfulness, that' s what love means,
Days may come, days may go, time passes fast,
But our love grows stronger still, long may it last.

Appendix 11

The Probus Song

Verse 1
Now that our youth has long since passed
Life is less urgent, not so fast,
We've time to sit and think at last
How best to live our lives.
Join us at Probus, meet with your friends,
Relax and be happy as Nature intends,
With such good companions your lifestyle extends,
Probus, the Club for you.

Verse 2
Life does not end at sixty-five,
We aim to show we're still alive,
We'll prove that we've not lost our drive,
Or our will to serve.
Join us at Probus, the time will speed by,
Revive your ambitions and reach for the sky,
You may not succeed but at least you can try,
Probus, the Club for you.

Appendix 12

Piccolo Pete and the Band

Verse 1
This is the tale of a band,
The best in all the land they told us,
Playing at all the gigs, their fans thought they were quite tremendous,
Pulling out all the stops, they soon became top of the pops,
And so began the band, the best in all the land.

Verse 2
First there was organist Fred,
Who was an expert with the pedals,
He was just superb and had earned a lot of medals,
Though not quite symphonic, his music was a tonic,
And he was one of the band,
The best in all the land.

Verse 3
Joey was on the percussion,
He was great but quite a boaster
'Til the day arrived when he fell off a roller coaster,
Tricky to play the drums without any fingers or thumbs,
And so he left the band, the best in all the land.

Verse 4
Bert Birkett strummed on the guitar,
Although at times he was moronic
His fingerwork was slick, his instrument was electronic
Then he had a short circuit – and that was the end of Bert Birkett,
So he was out of the band, the best in all the land.

continued...

Verse 5
Piccolo Pete was the star,
He had to show them who was master,
When the band played fast Piccolo Pete played rather faster,
But when he ran out of puff he decided he'd had enough,
And that was the end of the band, the best in all the land.

Appendix 13

I Wanna Go 'Ome

Verse 1
When I was a younger man the world was at my feet,
I was full of life and fancy free,
But now that I am older I think 'ome is 'ard to beat,
It's back to where I came from, that's for me.

CHORUS
I wanna go 'ome, I wanna go 'ome, take me back to dear old London Town,
I wanna go 'ome, I wanna go 'ome, 'ave a night out at the Rose and Crown,
You can keep Majorca and your sunny Spain, 'olidays abroad are not for me,
A week-end down at Brighton, never mind the rain, that's what
    I call going on a spree,
I wanna go 'ome, I wanna go 'ome, that's where I can be alone,
I've said goodbye to roamin', what's the use of moanin'?
I wanna go 'ome, that's what I'm saying,
I wanna go 'ome, that's where I'm staying,
I wanna go 'ome.

Verse 2
Though I've travelled round the world by land and sea and air,
And seen exotic countries by the score,
There is only one place that's great beyond compare,
And where I wanna stay forever more.

CHORUS
As above